Home To Home

The Step-By-Step Senior Housing Guide

Senior Planning Workbook
Local Edition

TO:

FROM:

Brad and Christy Brewer

&

Max Keller

Home To Home: The Step-By-Step Senior Housing Guide —
Senior Planning Workbook
Local Edition
ISBN: 978-1-7341665-5-2

© 2019 by Savior Publishing House LLC
2140 Hall Johnson Ste. 102-320
Grapevine, TX 76051
info@saviorpublishinghouse.com
817-527-8207

Brad Brewer and Christy Brewer
Kash4Homes, LLC
For more info, reach out to us at www.kash4homes.org, 636-442-1811, or bradandchristy@theseniorhousingbook.com.

No part of this book may be reproduced, distributed, or transmitted in any form or by any means, including photocopying, recording, or other electronic or mechanical methods, without the prior written permission of the publisher, except in the case of brief quotations embodied in critical reviews and certain other non-commercial uses permitted by copyright law.

Table of Contents

ACKNOWLEDGEMENTS IX
    DEDICATION XIII
    PREFACE: SENIOR PLANNING GUIDE OVERVIEW XV
        Workbook Goal xv
        What This Workbook Will Not Do xvi
        About the Publisher xvi
        Disclaimer xvii

INTRODUCTION 1

CHAPTER 1: STARTING LINE 3
    Chapter Goals 3
    Why Is This Important? 3
    Exercise: Step 1 — Contact Information (1.1) 4
    Exercise: Step 2 — Advisory Team (1.2) 5
    Exercise: Step 3 — Document Location 6
    Exercise: Step 4 — Document Details 7
        Banking (1.3) 7
        Real Estate (1.4) 8
        Insurance (1.5) 9
        Legal (1.6) 10
        Computer Passwords (1.7) 11
    Chapter Summary 12

CHAPTER 2: FINISH LINE 13
    Chapter Goals 13
    Why Is This Important? 13
    Setting Up Your Plan 14
        Checklist: Step 1 — Challenges 14
        Checklist: Step 2 — Health 14
        Checklist: Step 3 — Preferences 15
        Checklist: Step 4 — Housing 15
        Checklist: Step 5 — Relationships 16
        Checklist: Step 6 — Advisory Team 17
        Checklist: Step 7 — Smooth Transition 18
        Checklist: Step 8 — Personal Budget Checklist 19

    Exercise: Monthly Budget (2.1) 20
  STOP: READ THIS BEFORE MOVING ON 21
    Next Steps 21
  Chapter Summary 21

CHAPTER 3: SELLING YOUR HOME ROADMAP 23

  Chapter Goals 23
  Why Is This Important? 23
  Exercise: Home Condition (3.1) 23
  Exercise: Home Inventory (3.2) 24
  Three Ways to Sell Your Home Comparison 26
  The Three Ways to Sell Your Home 27
  1. Sell the Home with a Real Estate Agent 27
    Benefits 27
    Ideal Customers 27
    Drawbacks 27
    Exercise: Step 1 — Real Estate Agent Questions (3.3) 28
    Exercise: Step 2 — Real Estate Agent Questions (3.4) 29
    Example: How Much Will You Really Make? 30
    Explanation of Selling Costs — Using an Agent 31
    Example of Selling Costs and Net Proceeds 32
  2. Update Your Home Before You Sell It 33
    Benefits 33
    Ideal Customers 33
    Drawbacks 33
    Exercise: Step 1 — Project Planning (3.5) 34
    Exercise: Step 2 — Contractor Questions (3.6) 35
    Exercise: Step 3 — Contractor Questions (3.7) 36
  3. Sell to an Investor 37
    Benefits 37
    Ideal Customers 37
    Drawbacks 37
    Exercise: Step 1 — Investor Questions (3.8) 38
    Exercise: Step 2 — Investor Questions (3.9) 39
  Chapter Summary 40

CHAPTER 4: KEEPING YOUR HOME ROADMAP 41

  Chapter Goals 41

Why Is This Important? *41*
Benefits of Solving Early *41*
    Exercise: Step 1 — Keeping Your Home Questions (4.1) 42
    Example: Monthly Home Budget 43
    Exercise: Step 1 — Monthly Home Budget (4.2) 44
    Exercise: Step 2 — Preparing for Large Expenses 45
    Exercise: Step 3 — Maintaining Major Home Systems (4.3) 46
    Retrofitting Your Home 47
    Checklist: Step 4 — Contractor Referral Check Questions (4.4) 48
    Contractor Tips (4.5) 49
    Bringing in Help: Medical and Personal Care 50
    Checklist: Step 5 — Home Agency Phone Interview Questions (4.6) 51
Chapter Summary *52*

CHAPTER 5: SENIOR HOUSING CHOICES ROADMAP 53

Chapter Goals *53*
Three Levels of Care *53*
1. Independent Living *54*
    Age-Restricted Communities 55
    Senior Apartments, Townhomes, and Garden Homes 56
    Move-In with a Family Member 57
    Renting a Room to Live In or Renting Out a Room in Your House .. 58
2. Assisted Living *59*
    Assisted Living: Corporate Location 60
    Residential Assisted Living Facilities 61
    Memory Care 62
3. Nursing Care *63*
    Nursing Homes 64
    CCRC: Continuing Care Retirement Communities 65
Chapter Summary *66*

CHAPTER 6: SENIOR HOUSING ROADMAP 67

Chapter Goals *67*
Three Steps to Finding Your Ideal Facility *67*
1. Needs and Wants *68*
    Exercise: Step 1 — Setting Up Your Plan (6.1) 69
    Exercise: Step 1 — Setting Up Your Plan Cont. (6.1) 70

  Exercise: Step 2 — Your Team (6.2) 71
  Checklist: Step 3 — Closest Advisor Questions (6.3) 72
  Exercise: Step 4 — Your Budget (6.4) 73
  Exercise: Step 5 — Other Planning Questions (6.5) 74
  Exercise: Step 5 — Other Planning Questions Cont. (6.5) 75
 2. Identify and Interview 76
  Exercise: Step 6 — Before You Call Questions (Identify) (6.6) 77
  Checklist: Step 7 — Call the Facility (Phone Interview) (6.7) 78
  Checklist: Step 8 — Tour Questions (In Person Interview) (6.8) 79
 3. Decision 81
  Checklist: Step 9 — Facility Comparison Part 1 (6.9) 82
  Checklist: Step 10 — Facility Comparison Part 2 (6.10) 83
 Next Steps: Tips 84
 Reach Out to Us for Help 85
 Chapter Summary 85

CHAPTER 7: PAYING FOR SENIOR HOUSING 87
 Chapter Goals 87
 Medicare 88
 Medicare Supplemental Insurance 88
 Medicaid 89
 Long-Term Care Insurance 90
 Reverse Mortgage 91
 Other Ways to Pay 92
 Other Resources 92
 Things to Watch Out for 92
 Reach Out to Us 93
 Chapter Summary 93

CHAPTER 8: SPECIAL CHALLENGES FOR FAMILY MEMBERS OF SENIORS 95
 Chapter Goals 95
  Lack of Appreciation from Seniors Being Taken Care of by Family Members 96
  Strained Relationships Before Care Began 96
  Caring for Seniors with Memory Issues 96
  Major Health Issues 97
  Financial Issues 97

    One Sibling Doing All the Work or Blocking Other People from Seeing the Senior 98
    Taking Care of Senior Parents while Still Taking Care of Children at Home 98
    Feeling Guilty for Putting Your Parents in Senior Living Facilities 99
    Each Adult Child Sibling Sees the Senior's Needs Differently 99
    The Senior Does Not Want to Admit That They Need Help 100
    How to Pay for Senior Care 100
    Caring for Both Parents at Once 101
  In Closing *101*

APPENDIX 103

What Is Included in This Section *103*
Contact Information (1.1) *104*
Advisory Team (1.2) *105*
    Banking (1.3) 106
    Real Estate (1.4) 107
    Insurance (1.5) 108
    Legal (1.6) 109
    Computer Passwords (1.7) 110
Exercise: Home Condition (3.1) *114*
Exercise: Home Inventory (3.2) *115*
Exercise: Home Inventory (3.2) *116*
    Real Estate Agent Questions (3.3) 117
    Real Estate Agent Questions (3.3) 118
    Real Estate Agent Questions (3.3) 119
    Real Estate Agent Questions (3.3) 120
    Real Estate Agent Questions (3.3) 121
    Real Estate Agent Questions (3.4) 122
    Real Estate Agent Questions (3.4) 123
    Real Estate Agent Questions (3.4) 124
    Real Estate Agent Questions (3.4) 125
    Real Estate Agent Questions (3.4) 126
    Project Planning (3.5) 127
    Project Planning (3.5) 128
    Contractor Questions (3.6) 129
    Contractor Questions (3.6) 130

Contractor Questions (3.6) 131
Contractor Questions (3.6) 132
Contractor Questions (3.6) 133
Contractor Questions (3.7) 134
Contractor Questions (3.7) 135
Contractor Questions (3.7) 136
Contractor Questions (3.7) 137
Contractor Questions (3.7) 138
Investor Questions (3.8) 139
Investor Questions (3.8) 140
Investor Questions (3.8) 141
Investor Questions (3.8) 142
Investor Questions (3.8) 143
Investor Questions (3.9) 144
Investor Questions (3.9) 145
Investor Questions (3.9) 146
Investor Questions (3.9) 147
Investor Questions (3.9) 148
Keeping Your Home Questions (4.1) 149
Monthly Home Budget (4.2) 150
Monthly Home Budget (4.2) 151
Maintaining Major Home Systems (4.3) 152
Maintaining Major Home Systems (4.3) 153
Contractor Referral Check Questions (4.4) 154
Contractor Referral Check Questions (4.4) 155
Contractor Referral Check Questions (4.4) 156
Contractor Referral Check Questions (4.4) 157
Contractor Referral Check Questions (4.4) 158
Contractor Tips (4.5) 159
Contractor Tips (4.5) 160
Contractor Tips (4.5) 161
Contractor Tips (4.5) 162
Contractor Tips (4.5) 163
Home Agency Phone Interview Questions (4.6) 164
Home Agency Phone Interview Questions (4.6) 165
Home Agency Phone Interview Questions (4.6) 166
Home Agency Phone Interview Questions (4.6) 167

Home Agency Phone Interview Questions (4.6) 168
Setting Up Your Plan (6.1) 169
Setting Up Your Plan Cont. (6.1) 170
Your Team (6.2) 171
Closest Advisor Questions (6.3) 172
Your Budget (6.4) 173
Other Planning Questions (6.5) 174
Other Planning Questions Cont. (6.5) 175
Before You Call Questions (Identify) (6.6) 176
Before You Call Questions (Identify) (6.6) 177
Before You Call Questions (Identify) (6.6) 178
Before You Call Questions (Identify) (6.6) 179
Before You Call Questions (Identify) (6.6) 180
Call the Facility (Phone Interview) (6.7) 181
Call the Facility (Phone Interview) (6.7) 182
Call the Facility (Phone Interview) (6.7) 183
Call the Facility (Phone Interview) (6.7) 184
Call the Facility (Phone Interview) (6.7) 185
Tour Questions (In Person Interview) (6.8) 186
Tour Questions (In Person Interview) (6.8) 188
Tour Questions (In Person Interview) (6.8) 190
Tour Questions (In Person Interview) (6.8) 192
Tour Questions (In Person Interview) (6.8) 194
Facility Comparison Part 1 (6.9) 196
Facility Comparison Part 1 (6.9) 197
Facility Comparison Part 1 (6.9) 198
Facility Comparison Part 1 (6.9) 199
Facility Comparison Part 1 (6.9) 200
Facility Comparison Part 2 (6.10) 201
Facility Comparison Part 2 (6.10) 202
Facility Comparison Part 2 (6.10) 203

ABOUT US 205
  Brad and Christy Brewer 205
  Max Keller 207

Acknowledgements

This book could not have been possible without the unwavering and unconditional love and support of our families. It is through their dedication and teachings that we have learned the meaning and value of love, respect, and caring for others. We will forever be grateful for their presence in our lives, and their role in the success and happiness we experience today.

Brad and Christy Brewer

Senior Planning Workbook

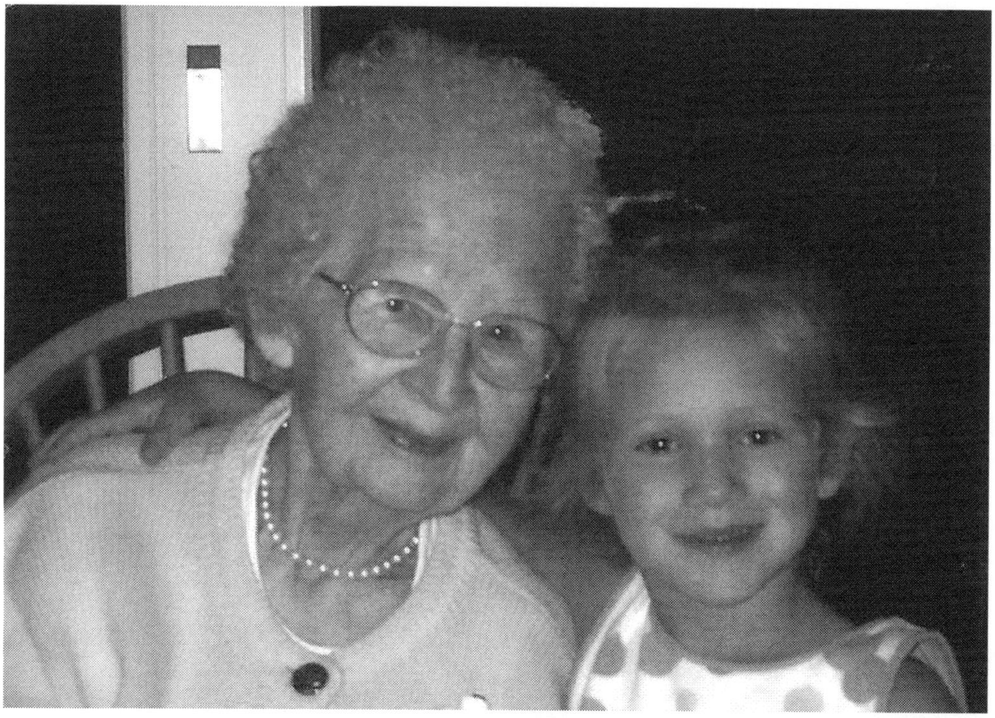

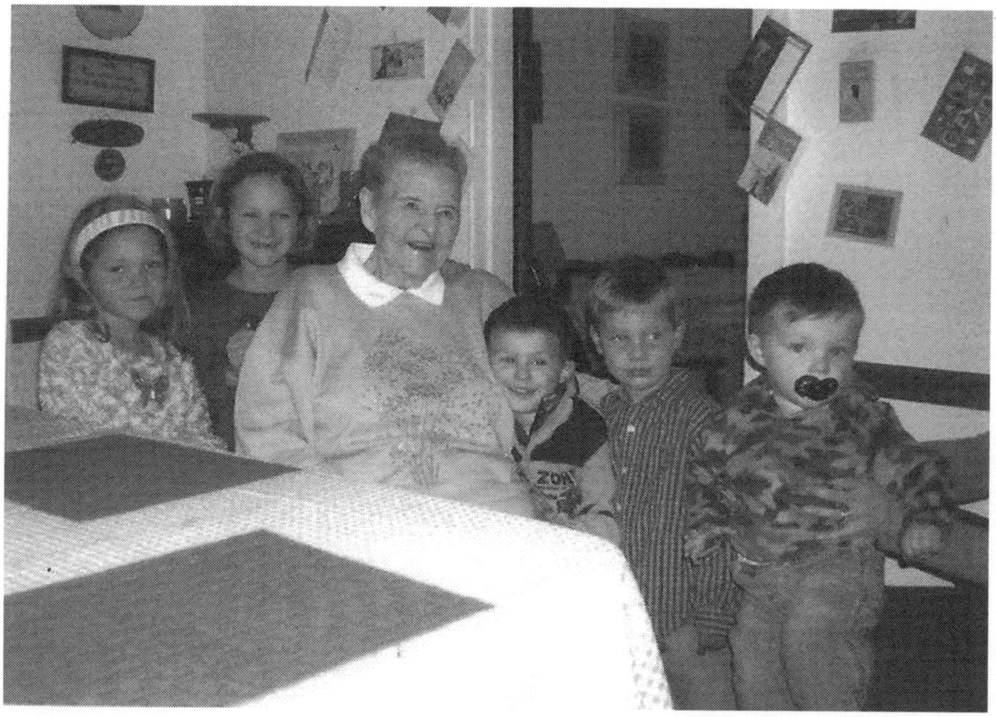

Dedication

This workbook is dedicated to my wonderful family, whose support and trust have allowed me to serve many seniors in their housing journey.

I also want to thank God for the tools and talents he has given me to serve the many.

Max Keller

"My people will live in peaceful dwelling places, in secure homes, in undisturbed places of rest" (**Isaiah 32:18).**

Preface: Senior Planning Guide Overview

This workbook is an extension to *Home to Home: The Step-By-Step Senior Housing Guide*, which you may have already read. If you do not have a copy, please reach out to us at www.kash4homes.org, 636-442-1811, or bradandchristy@theseniorhousingbook.com.

Workbook Goal

The goal is for this workbook to be your guide from now until you leave this Earth. It has been designed as a training guide that will shine more light on each chapter from *Home To Home*.

This workbook will delve deeper into the most important parts of the book so that you and your family will have a comprehensive plan for your senior housing needs. However, the workbook does not negate the need to have an expert team member — such as a financial advisor, an attorney, an accountant, a doctor, and family members — within your circle of counsel. Instead, this workbook serves to compliment these professions by raising questions that you can review with each of them.

We can guarantee you this: if you are willing to fill this entire guide out with your team and come up with a plan, you will feel more at ease with your Senior Housing Plan.

This plan extends beyond just housing to also touch on your legacy — how are you going to be remembered after you leave the Earth? Wouldn't it be better to be more purposeful with your goals and wishes instead of leaving everything to chance?

The goal of this guide is to add purpose to your planning. If you suddenly get sick or have a drastic change in health, a completed guide will be the roadmap for your family members to follow — what a blessing that would be! If disaster strikes (and we hope it never does), you will be prepared; you can hand this plan to your family, and they will be able to help you reach your goals.

We are looking forward to sharing this blessing with you. It is going to take a lot of work, but we know that it is worth it, and we know that you feel the same way.

What This Workbook Will Not Do

This workbook will not do the planning for you.

You and your team have to open the book, read each line, think about your plan, talk to each other, and write your plan down. In order for your plan to turn into reality, you have to take the completed plan (Step 1) and then put it into action (Step 2).

We cannot do all this for you. It takes a lot of people working together, but most of the effort is going to come from you. The good news is that we have tackled the hardest part for you, which was organizing each section and formulating the tough questions that need to be answered.

About the Publisher

Savior Publishing House LLC is a national publisher that partners with local experts in real estate who have the desire to serve their clients before themselves; in this sense, we only work with the leading experts in a given area. The local author of your book wants to serve their community and run a successful business. If you find value in this and other books, please pass them on to people you know, like, and trust. Our company's mission is to help over 1,000,000 seniors and their adult children formulate the best possible plan. Thanks to a great network of local experts, we will continue to make a difference through knowledge and education.

Disclaimer

The information in this book is not meant to replace the advice of a certified professional. Please consult a licensed advisor in matters relating to your personal and professional well-being including your mental, emotional and physical health, finances, business, legal matters, and education. The views and opinions expressed throughout the book are those of the author and do not necessarily reflect the views or opinions of any other agency, organization, employer, publisher, or company. Since we are critically-thinking human beings, the views of the author are always subject to change at any time. Any references to past performance may not be indicative of future results. No warranties or guarantees are expressed or implied by the publisher's choice to include any of the content in this volume.

If you choose to attempt any of the methods mentioned in this book, the author and publisher advise you to take full responsibility for your results. The author and publisher are not liable for any damages or negative consequences from any treatment, action, application, or preparation to any person reading or following the information in this book.

Brad and Christy Brewer and Max Keller

Introduction

We are committed to bettering the lives of our senior generation, and pride ourselves on our core values of honesty, dependability, and compassion. There have been many poignant experiences in our real-estate career that have left a lasting impression, but one in particular stands out for me:

Pat found my number on one of our marketing pamphlets and called me. She had been in long-term care following surgery and had just returned home but didn't think she should be living alone anymore. She didn't have any family in the area that were able to help her. Over the course of the following weeks, we talked regularly and developed a friendship; she often mentioned how grateful she was for all we were doing for her, particularly as she didn't have family who could help her. It took several weeks for her to find an assisted living facility but, during that time, we talked every few days. When a facility finally became available, and she was ready to close on the sale of her house, Christy and I drove our utility trailer to her home and helped her pack up her belongings, loaded our car, and accompanied Pat to her new assisted living home. On arrival, we helped Pat unpack and settle into her new room; from that moment on, Pat was so busy socializing and participating in various activities, she was difficult to get ahold of.

Helping Pat find and settle into a living situation where she was able to feel supported and happy, gave us an overwhelming sense of satisfaction. I genuinely enjoyed every minute I spent talking and listening to her. Knowing that we provided her with reassurance and support during a difficult time was extremely rewarding—we take an immense amount of pride in helping others.

My passion for real estate started in college, when a good friend of mine and I purchased a dilapidated mobile home across the street from where we were living. We gave ourselves 30 days to renovate it and put it back on the property market for resale. We stayed within our budget and timeframe, sold the renovated property for a profit, and I have been hooked on real estate ever since.

Seniors have so much knowledge to share and so many stories to tell about their past. Christy's passion for working with seniors comes from over 20 years working in a rehabilitation, long term care setting and as a caregiver. I have attended countless meetings where families struggle to find the answers to so many questions: What amount of care is needed, where should we look, what do we do about the house, how do we manage the finances? The process always seemed to carry so much stress and emotional upheaval for all parties involved, and I always felt that there must be a better way to help seniors and their families through such a difficult time.

Christy and I love what we do and thrive on every day being a new day, with different tasks and responsibilities, and an opportunity to meet and help new people. In addition to our wonderful clients, I relish the fulfillment and satisfaction that completing a renovation brings.

In working with the senior community, we have been fortunate enough to spend time with many of our clients, listening to their stories, and helping them to make an important and often difficult transition in their lives. Our plan for the future is to build a residential, assisted living home that gives our seniors more choice when they reach the stage that they need help with their day-to-day lives.

Chapter 1: Starting Line

Chapter Goals

The goal of this chapter is for you to start organizing your documents so that we can create a plan later in the workbook. One of the biggest struggles our customers run into occurs when a family member gets sick and no one can find any paperwork, access important computer files, or even know what type of accounts their family member possesses.

The best thing you can do for your family is to fill out Chapter 1 completely, put the guide in a secure place (such as a small fireproof safe in your home), and tell a member of your advisory team where you kept the book.

Why Is This Important?

In order to formulate your plan, you will have to get organized. Too many families end up having to sort through piles of paperwork and spend hundreds of hours making phone calls just to get the basic information to address their loved one's situation.

After completing this workbook, your family members can look at it as a helping hand if it is ever needed. This workbook will also help you to plan out what it is you want during your golden years.

For more information, reach out to us at www.kash4homes.org, 636-442-1811, or bradandchristy@theseniorhousingbook.com.

"It wasn't raining when Noah built the ark." — Howard Ruff

Senior Planning Workbook

Exercise: Step 1 — Contact Information (1.1)

Directions: Fill out the contact information below.

Senior Name: _____

Senior's Spouse's Name: _____

Address: _____

Phone: _____

Email: _____

Today's Date: _____

Emergency Contacts

Contact #1

Name: _____

Relation: _____

Phone Number: _____

Alternative Phone Number: _____

Email Address: _____

Contact #2

Name: _____

Relation: _____

Phone Number: _____

Alternative Phone Number: _____

Email Address: _____

Exercise: Step 2 — Advisory Team (1.2)

Directions: List Your Professional Team and Contact Info	
Professional	**Contact Info**
Attorney:	
Financial Advisor:	
CPA:	
Medical Team:	
Medical Team:	
Other Advisor:	
Other Advisor:	

Closest Advisor: This could be the executor of your will or estate, a close family member, or another member of your advisory team. Choose this person carefully. Make sure that this person will execute your wishes and is looking out for your best interests. If there is no one in your family that would fit this role, an attorney can (if established ahead of time).

Notes:

_____

_____

_____

Exercise: Step 3 — Document Location

The #1 issue our seniors' adult children run into is: "Where are all the documents? My mom or dad is really sick or in the hospital, and I have no idea where to find any of their paperwork."

The best gift you can give your family is organized paperwork.

Tip: Buy a small fireproof safe and keep this completed workbook and ALL the documents from the proceeding checklists in it. Another place could be a safe deposit box. You can also consider sharing a copy of this completed workbook with your top advisor.

Homework: Call the contacts you listed on the previous page and let them know where this completed workbook will be kept.

Notes:
_____
_____
_____

Exercise: Step 4 — Document Details

Banking (1.3)

\multicolumn{4}{c	}{Banking and Investment Information}
Type	Company Name	Account Number	Phone Number
Checking			
Checking			
Savings			
Savings			
Investment			
Investment			
Other			
Other			
Other			
Other			

Homework: Print out all the statements from each of these accounts and put them in the same safe and secure place you will be keeping your workbook.

Senior Planning Workbook

Real Estate (1.4)

Primary Residence	
Property Address	
Paid Off?	(Circle One) YES NO
Name of Title Holder(s)	
Mortgage Company Information	
Company Name	
Phone Number	
Account Number	
2nd Mortgage (On Same Property)	
Company Name	
Phone Number	
Account Number	

Other Property	
Property Address	
Property Paid Off?	(Circle One) YES NO
Name of Title Holder(s)	
Mortgage Company Information	
Company Name	
Phone Number	
Account Number	
2nd Mortgage (On Same Property)	
Company Name	
Phone Number	
Account Number	

Homework: Print out all the statements from each of these accounts and put them in the same safe and secure place you will be keeping your workbook.

Insurance (1.5)

Insurance Provider Information			
Type	**Company Name**	**Policy Number**	**Phone Number**
Health			
Life			
Disability			
Long-Term Care			
Homeowner's			
Auto			
Other			
Other			

Homework: Print out each of these policies and put them in the same safe and secure place you will be keeping your workbook.

Notes:
_____
_____
_____

Legal (1.6)

Legal Document Information		
Document Type	**Have You Created This Document? (Yes or No)**	**Date Created**
Medical Directive		
Durable Power of Attorney for Healthcare and HIPAA Release		
Durable Power of Attorney for Finances		
Revocable Living Trust		
Will		

Homework: Make a copy of all these documents and keep them in your secure location.

Notes:
_____
_____
_____

Computer Passwords (1.7)

Tip: For added security, look into getting an online password vault that will store all your passwords for you—our company uses *1Password*. You will be able to save all your passwords and create vaults for your family members so that you can give them access to your accounts if needed.

Website	User Name	Password

Chapter Summary

In this chapter, we have identified the most important documents you need to make accessible to your family members and advisory team. Which documents were the most challenging to locate? How much more difficult do you think it would have been for a family member or advisory team member to access that information in the event of something happening to you?

Now that you have all these items organized and stored in a secure location, we are ready to move on to the next chapter.

Chapter 2: Finish Line

Chapter Goals

The goal of this chapter is to answer some questions and get you thinking about what the future will look like, which we plan to achieve by going through a series of "what if" scenarios in order to see what your answers are at this present time. Outlining what your desires are will help you, your heirs, and your advisory team to make the best choices when necessary. By the end of this chapter, you should have a good framework to make the decisions that will be required by the content in the following chapters.

Why Is This Important?

It is important to map out exactly where you or your senior wants to be as you transition into senior housing. Your ideal destination has a great deal to do with the type of lifestyle you envision living.

Notes:

_____

_____

_____

Setting Up Your Plan

Checklist: Step 1 — Challenges

☐ Are there any current problems or challenges you are facing?

☐ What is the single biggest problem you are trying to solve?

☐ How soon do you expect to move into a senior housing facility?

☐ How will you know when it is time to make a decision?

Checklist: Step 2 — Health

☐ If your health were to change quickly, what would your preference be (rank in order 1, 2, and 3)?

_____ Have someone move in to help you
_____ Hire someone to help you
_____ Move somewhere else

☐ What types of personal care services do you need now or want to be available (e.g., dressing, mobility help, laundry, bathing, and food)?

☐ What type of medical care services do you need now or want to be available (e.g., treatments, specialty care, medicine, or diabetes care)?

☐ If you are thinking about moving across the city, state, or country, will you need to find a new doctor or other professionals?

Checklist: Step 3 — Preferences

☐ What has prompted you to start this search?

☐ What geographical location do you want to live in?

☐ If price were no object, where would you want to live?

☐ What amenities would you like to have available (e.g., entertainment, recreation, food, pool, classes, and transportation)?

☐ Are there any other needs or wants you have not mentioned yet that are important to you?

☐ Do you want to be close to a church or place of worship? Which one?

Checklist: Step 4 — Housing

☐ Do you have a specific housing need right now? If so, what is it (i.e., independent, assisted, nursing, or specialty)?

☐ What type of environment do you want to live in (e.g., private, community, social, private room, shared room, private house, or first floor)?

☐ How long will it take to sell your home and/or move?

☐ Would you prefer to move into a facility that has all the care options available, from independent to nursing, or would you be fine moving to a new facility if you needed more care?

☐ If you are moving into a furnished facility, what is the plan for your current furniture and personal belongings?

☐ Will you need to rent a storage facility? If so, where?

Checklist: Step 5 — Relationships

☐ If you are currently living with a spouse and they pass away, would you want to stay in your home or move? Why?

☐ Are you married?

☐ Do you currently live with anyone else?

☐ If you move, where is your current house partner (e.g., friend, family, or spouse) going to live?

☐ Do those in your circle have any present concerns regarding your health, safety, or overall happiness (please document the response from their perspective)?

☐ What problems or challenges is your top advisor facing (please document the response from their perspective)?

☐ If your top advisor is a family member, is moving in with them or anyone else in your family an option (please document the response from their perspective)?

☐ Is there a friend or family member you want to live close to?

☐ If you plan to give items from your home away to family members, have you let your family members know?

☐ Will you get input from your family members before you give them any of your personal belongings?

☐ When you give a family member or friend your personal belongings, are the items theirs to keep or are you just letting them store them for you?

Checklist: Step 6 — Advisory Team

☐ Is your advisory team part of your planning process?

☐ What is important to the members of your advisory team? Ask them if you have not already, e.g., "I am creating a Senior Housing Plan that I expect to begin following (fill in the date, for example, next month, next year, or ten years). What is important to you?"

☐ Ask your advisory team, "Is there anything else you want me to consider as I am creating my plan?"

Senior Planning Workbook

Checklist: Step 7 — Smooth Transition

☐ If there is a health or mobility issue, who is the caretaker or assistant going to be?

☐ What steps will you follow to find the right caretaker to help you in your home?

☐ Who is going to help with the home maintenance?

☐ How is this home going to be passed on?

☐ Who will take future ownership of your home and when will it happen?

☐ Who will be in charge of this process?

Notes:

_____
_____
_____

Checklist: Step 8 — Personal Budget Checklist

❏ Do you use a monthly budget?

❏ What monthly amount can you afford for senior housing and care expenses?

❏ What financial sources are available to pay for senior housing?

❏ If you do not need senior housing right now, have you inquired about long-term care insurance?

❏ Do you expect family members to help pay for your housing? If so, how much do they plan to contribute?

❏ If you plan to sell your home, how much do you expect to receive?

Notes:
_____
_____
_____

Senior Planning Workbook

Exercise: Monthly Budget (2.1)

Directions: Fill out this sample budget using your current income and expenses and then total up each section. When each section has been totaled, subtract the total of each expense section from your total income — this will show you your monthly surplus (extra) or deficit (shortfall).

Income	Monthly	Medical Expenses	Monthly
Wages from Employment		Health Insurance	
Social Security		Regular Prescriptions	
401K or IRA Income		Out-of-Pocket	
Pension Benefit		**Medical Total**	
Rental Property Income			
Other		**Personal Expenses**	**Monthly**
Income Total		Clothing	
		Toiletries	
Housing Expenses	**Monthly**	Miscellaneous	
Rent/Mortgage/Taxes		Movies/Books	
Maintenance/Lawn		Cable TV	
Electric/Gas		Travel	
Water/Sewer/Garbage		**Personal Total**	
Phone/Internet			
Housing Total		**Debt**	**Monthly**
		Credit Card Payments	
Food/Car Expenses	**Monthly**	Personal Loan Payments	
Groceries		**Debt Total**	
Restaurants			
Car Payment/Insurance		**Total Monthly Income**	
Gasoline		**Total Monthly Expenses**	
Car Repairs		**Deficit or Surplus**	
Other			
Food/Car Total			

20

STOP: READ THIS BEFORE MOVING ON

At this point, you should have some important items documented and organized, and you should have taken a current inventory of where you are currently with your planning and what you want the future to look like.

Next Steps

By now, you should have made the decision to either sell your home or keep it for the time being. Based on your decision, select *Chapter 3: Selling Your Home Roadmap* or *Chapter 4: Keeping Your Home Roadmap* to determine the appropriate planning process for you.

There are several options regarding senior housing (see Chapters 5 and 6) — you need to move someone now, you need to move them soon, or you need to move them later (down the road). Go through all the steps in Chapters 5 and 6. You will either be able to use these chapters to pick the right fit for you and your family right now or you will have some choices and plans made for them when or if the time comes.

If you have filled out everything up to this point, congratulations! You are 90% more prepared than the rest of America. You are in the top 10%!!! Now, it is time for you to be in the top 1%. Continue and enjoy!

Chapter Summary

Review each checklist. What was your biggest takeaway from each one? Did they educate you on outcomes you had not anticipated? Did the "what if" scenarios help you to get better clarity on where you are and what you need to do in order to position yourself for the future you desire?

Your discoveries in this chapter are the foundations for what we will be covering in the following chapters. By doing so, you have successfully added one more vital element to your Senior Housing Plan.

For more information reach out to us at www.kash4homes.org, 636-442-1811, or bradandchristy@theseniorhousingbook.com.

Chapter 3: Selling Your Home Roadmap

Chapter Goals

The goal of this chapter is to guide you in the decision-making process if you decide that, based upon the discoveries you made in Chapter 2, letting your property go is the best option.

Why Is This Important?

There can be many reasons why someone may decide to sell their home, but the one that we run into most is a change in health. When someone no longer has the mobility or confidence to live at home, they often sell their home and move out. If that person does not have an appropriate support network or people who can move in with them, it is wise to make this change.

Exercise: Home Condition (3.1)

When was the last time your home was remodeled or updated?

(This can help you figure out the value of your home).

Date Updated	Updates Made	Amount Spent

Exercise: Home Inventory (3.2)

If you sell your home, what items do you plan to bring with you to your new home or apartment?

(Take a few minutes to think about the items in your home and what your plans for them are).

Item Description	Keep or Pass On?	If Pass On, To Whom?

If you have items that will not move with you and you do not want to pass on, what will you do with them?

Garage Sale?   YES   NO

Tip: You may need to call the city to get a permit.

☐ Who will help you with the sale?

Estate Sale?   YES   NO

☐ What company do you plan to use?

Donate?   YES   NO

☐ What organizations do you want to donate your items to?

Remember that some investor buyers will allow you to leave the items you will not be moving with at the home for no additional charge.

Notes:
_____
_____
_____

Three Ways to Sell Your Home Comparison

Agent – Ideal Customer	Agent – Pros	Agent – Cons
Designed for customers who want a traditional sale	Usually the highest price option (depending on condition)	Getting the house ready to sell
		Showing the home while you live there
Have time to invest in the closing process		Making repairs and upgrades
	If highly qualified, the agent can be added to your advisory team	Passing the home inspection
Homes have been partially or fully updated		Longer closing time
		Working with an inexperienced agent

Update – Ideal Customer	Update – Pros	Update – Cons
Customer who has money to invest in their home	Has the potential to make more than the other two options	Not recommended for most people
Not in a hurry to sell		Incorrect repairs/updates = wasted time and money
Contractor background or has access to contractors		Dealing with contractors
		Time consuming

Investor – Ideal Customer	Investor – Pros	Investor – Cons
Customer does not have a lot of money to put into the house for repairs or updates	Quick closing	Lower price, depending on the condition of the home
House is outdated and in average to poor condition	No repairs needed	
Needs or wants a quick closing	Less headaches	Inexperienced investors

The Three Ways to Sell Your Home

1. Sell the Home with a Real Estate Agent

Benefits

Someone who is buying a home to live in will usually pay the most.

Ideal Customers

This is designed for customers who want a traditional sale and have time to invest in the closing process. Ideal homes have been partially or fully updated to current standards.

Drawbacks

This method takes longer than an investor purchase, with associated challenges including: Getting the house ready to sell, showing the home to buyers while you are still living in it, making repairs and upgrades to the home that match buyers' expectations, coordinating a closing date, closings may not always happen on time or can get cancelled, and passing the home inspection after the house is under contract.

Senior Planning Workbook

Exercise: Step 1 — Real Estate Agent Questions (3.3)

(Before You Call)

☐ Is your home updated to current standards? YES   NO

☐ Does your home need any repairs?   YES   NO

(If yes, fill out the table below).

Part of the Home	Repairs Needed	Estimated Price

☐ When do you need to sell your home by?

☐ How long will you need to move out of your home and take care of your possessions?

☐ If your home sells faster than your new home is ready, who would you stay with or where would you move to temporarily (less than 30 days).

Exercise: Step 2 — Real Estate Agent Questions (3.4)

(In Person)

☐ How long have you been in business?

☐ Are you full time or part time?

☐ Is the real estate agent you are considering related to you? If yes, how would a negative real estate transaction impact on your family relationships?

☐ What neighborhood do you specialize in?

☐ Have you helped buy or sell a house in this neighborhood in the last 12 months?

☐ How much is my house worth in its current condition? How did you come up with that number?

☐ Based on the market and this neighborhood, how long will it take to sell my home?

☐ When we get an offer, what types of repairs, closing cost contributions, or price reductions are possible?

☐ Can I contact your **references**?

Senior Planning Workbook

Example: How Much Will You Really Make?

There are hidden costs to selling a home, and the following example — based on a customer we recently worked with — will walk you through some of these. However, the exact costs and percentages will vary depending on many factors.

Betty was considering selling her home and moving to a 55+ community, with homes in her area selling for as much as $245,000 at the time. If everything was brought up to code and updated to current standards, Betty's house, which was on the smaller side based on its size, would have sold for around $215,000.

Not much remodeling had been done to the home for 30 years. Betty's real estate agent was not 100% sure it would even get $175,000 in its current condition but wanted to list the home and test the market — Betty agreed.

On the next page are some examples of expenses or price reductions that had to happen to get the home sold.

30

Explanation of Selling Costs — Using an Agent	%
List Price/Market Value	100%
Real Estate Commissions	-6%
Buyer's Discount	-4%
Home Repairs	-2%
Monthly Mortgage and Maintenance	-3%
Standard Closing Costs and Misc. Fees	-3%
Final Net Proceeds	82%

- **List Price**: The price your home is listed for sale. You may get above or below the list price depending on your home, your location, the season, and the market.

- **Real Estate Commissions**: This is the price a seller pays to sell their home. Using 6% in our example, 3% of the sales price of the home gets paid to the listing agent for their work in selling the home, while 3% gets paid to the buyer's agent who works with the person purchasing your home.

- **Buyer's Discount**: This would be a discount on the sales price if your home was priced too high, in poor condition, or was not selling fast enough.

- **Home Repairs**: The number of repairs that would need to be made before the buyer will accept the purchase.

- **Monthly Mortgage and Maintenance**: During the closing process, you still have to maintain the home and make the mortgage payments.

- **Standard Closing Costs**: Fees that could be paid by the seller at closing.

- **Final Net Proceeds**: The final amount you receive minus liens and taxes owed.

Senior Planning Workbook

Example of Selling Costs and Net Proceeds

Explanation of Selling Costs — Agent	%	Example
List Price/Market Value	100%	$175,000
Real Estate Commissions	-6%	-$10,500
Buyer's Discount	-4%	-$7,000
Home Repairs	-2%	-$3,500
Monthly Mortgage and Maintenance	-3%	-$5,250
Standard Closing Costs and Misc. Fees	-3%	-$5,250
Final Net Proceeds	82%	$143,500

Betty started out on her selling journey by listening to neighbors with larger fixed-up houses who were selling them for $245,000. By the time the size, condition, selling costs, and price reductions were taken into consideration, Betty ended up making only $143,500 on her home in this example (not including mortgages and taxes owed).

2. Update Your Home Before You Sell It
Example of Selling Costs and Net Proceeds

Benefits

If the correct rehab plan is chosen, the seller finds great contractors, and everything follows the schedule, the seller can make more money from the sale of their home than options #1 or #3.

Ideal Customers

These are customers who have money to invest in their home and are not in a hurry to sell. Ideal customers will either have a contractor background or have access to contractors.

Drawbacks

There are many, and therefore we do not recommend this option for most people. If the incorrect repairs/updates are chosen for the area, the investment can be wasted. Dealing with contractors is challenging, and doing the work yourself can be very time-consuming, sometimes taking months or even a year longer than expected to complete big projects.

Senior Planning Workbook

Exercise: Step 1 — Project Planning (3.5)

(Before You Do the Work)

☐ How much money are you willing to invest in updating your home before selling it?

☐ How will you pay for remodeling your home?

(Circle any that apply)

Cash	Credit Card	Reverse Mortgage	Home Equity Line of Credit
Family Loan	Bank Loan	Other	Home Equity Mortgage

☐ What updates would your home need to be up to current remodeling standards?

Part of the Home	Update Needed	Estimated Price

☐ How soon do you need to get the repairs completed?

☐ Do you need a contractor referral? If yes, you can call our office at 636-442-1811 for a referral or if you have any questions you need answered.

Exercise: Step 2 — Contractor Questions (3.6)

(Before You Do the Work)

Directions: Fill this out before you meet the contractor.

Company: _____

Representative Name: _____

Phone: _____

Email: _____

- ❏ How did you find out about this contractor?

- ❏ What services does this contractor offer?

- ❏ Is the contractor insured and bonded?

- ❏ Does the contractor have any specialties?

- ❏ What do the online reviews say about this contractor (see Google, Facebook, and the Better Business Bureau)?

Notes:

_____

_____

_____

Senior Planning Workbook

Exercise: Step 3 — Contractor Questions (3.7)

(In Person)

Directions: Fill this out when you meet with the contractor.

Company: _____

Representative Name: _____

Phone: _____

Email: _____

- ❏ What are the core values of your company?

- ❏ What kind of work do you specialize in?

- ❏ Do you perform background checks on your staff?

- ❏ How do you come up with your pricing?

- ❏ Do you have references I can call?

- ❏ When are you available to start work?

- ❏ What type of payment schedule do you follow?

Notes:

_____

_____

_____

3. Sell to an Investor

Benefits

Selling to an investor does have benefits. Customers that are a good fit for this want or need to sell their homes quickly. Typically, this involves a completed closing in less than 30 days from when they go under contract.

Ideal Customers

Ideal customers would be those who do not have a lot of money to put into the house for repairs or updates. Other instances are where the house is usually in rough shape or has a fair amount of deferred maintenance.

Drawbacks

If the home is mostly or fully updated, the purchase price will usually be lower than if the seller uses a real estate agent.

Senior Planning Workbook

Exercise: Step 1 — Investor Questions (3.8)

(Before You Do the Work)

Directions: Fill this out before you meet an investor-buyer.

☐ Are the mortgages, taxes, or any other liens late?

☐ Is there an impending foreclosure deadline?

☐ Is there a recent or impending bankruptcy?

☐ Is everyone on the title present and ready to sign the purchase agreement?

☐ Are there any family members or other advisors you want to include in this decision?

☐ What is the payoff amount for your mortgage?

☐ Come up with three prices for your home:

    ☐ Price you would really like   _____
    ☐ Price you would accept   _____
    ☐ Your absolute minimum price   _____

Exercise: Step 2 — Investor Questions (3.9)

(In Person)

Directions: Fill this out when you meet with the investor-buyer.

- ☐ How did you come up with a fair price for the home?

- ☐ How are you going to pay for the house? Do you have a proof-of-funds letter?

- ☐ If I perform repairs on the house, will that increase the value of the home?

- ☐ In what condition can we leave the house in if we sell it to you?

- ☐ When can we close?

- ☐ Do you have any references?

- ☐ Will you need access to the property?

- ☐ When will the utilities and insurance be cut off?

- ☐ What does the closing process look like?

- ☐ Who pays additional lawyer or closing costs?

Senior Planning Workbook

Chapter Summary

This chapter was written to serve the needs of those seniors who realize that their best option is selling their property.

We have looked closely at the three options you would face, including the benefits and drawbacks of each one. We also clearly described the ideal senior for each option in order to make it easy for you to identify which one would be the best fit for you.

The checklists provided will enable you to vet the people you will be working with based upon the option you selected. We recommend getting three bids for any work you want to do; therefore, by the time you select the real estate agent, contractor, or investor-buyer, you would have filled out three sets of checklists. Additional copies of the checklists have been provided at the back of this book in the Appendix.

By utilizing the checklists provided, you will now have clear answers from each person, which helps to streamline your decision-making process and gives you the confidence to move forward with whoever you selected.

For more information, reach out to us at www.kash4homes.org, 636-442-1811, or bradandchristy@theseniorhousingbook.com.

Chapter 4: Keeping Your Home Roadmap

Chapter Goals

If you and your team…

- think about each question;
- answer the questions; and
- review the checklists

…you will have a plan in place to keep your home by the end of this chapter, and your wishes and home legacy will be able to be communicated to your family.

Why Is This Important?

If you want to stay in your house but your health is failing, you will need support in order to make your house a safe place to live in.

If you want to pass your home on to your family when you are no longer living in it, you will need to plan for who the home is going to and how to set everything up.

Benefits of Solving Early

There are three major benefits of a well-thought-out plan to keep your home:

1. Maintaining the value of your home;
2. Getting the right help you need; and
3. Creating a smooth transition.

Senior Planning Workbook

Exercise: Step 1 — Keeping Your Home Questions (4.1)

(Before You Start Work)

☐ Have there been any recent event(s) that make keeping your home a concern or a challenge?

☐ If your health condition changes, how would you be able to stay in your home? What alterations would need to be made to your home?

☐ Do any family members want to buy your home? If so, who?

☐ If someone in the family wants to buy the home if it was to come up for sale, how will that person pay for the home?

☐ If the person plans on getting a mortgage to pay for your house, are they certain they will qualify for a loan?

☐ If your health changes and you lose mobility, who will maintain your home?

Example: Monthly Home Budget

1234 Affordable Dr. – 3/2/2 – 1,220 square feet – built 1976

Big backyard; not much maintenance carried out in the last five years.

Current Value of Home	$150,000	Interest Rate
1st Mortgage Loan Amount	$75,000	5%
2nd Mortgage Loan Amount	$10,000	8%
Condition (circle one)	Good – Average – Poor	

Expenses – Monthly	Typical Monthly Cost	Actual Monthly Cost
1st Mortgage Payment	Based on loan amount	$403.00
2nd Mortgage Payment	Based on loan amount	$73.00
Homeowners Insurance	1% of the home value/12	$125.00
Property Taxes	1%–3% of home value/12	$125.00
Maintenance	1%–3% of home value depending on age and condition/12	$375.00
HOA Fees	$0–$100+	$0.00
Utilities – Electric	$50–$250+	$125.00
Utilities – Gas	$25–$150+	$35.00
Utilities Water	$25–$125+	$40.00
Utilities Trash	$10–$40+	$15.00
Snow Removal	$0–$50+	$0.00
Lawn Care	$0–$150+	$100.00
	Total Monthly Budget	**$1,416.00**

Senior Planning Workbook

Exercise: Step 1 — Monthly Home Budget (4.2)

Directions: Fill in the information to calculate your current home budget.

Address _____

Bedrooms _____ Bathrooms _____ Garage _____

Square Feet _____ Year Built _____

Yard Size (circle one) small   medium   large

Current Value of Home		Interest Rate	
1st Mortgage Loan			
2nd Mortgage Loan			
Condition (circle one)	Good – Average – Poor		
Expenses – Monthly	Typical Monthly Cost	Actual Monthly Cost	
1st Mortgage Payment	Based on loan amount		
2nd Mortgage Payment	Based on loan amount		
Homeowners Insurance	1% of the home value/12		
Property Taxes	1%–3% of home value/12		
Maintenance	1%–3% of home value/12		
HOA Fees	$0–$100+		
Utilities – Electric	$50–$250+		
Utilities – Gas	$25–$150+		
Utilities – Water	$25–$125+		
Utilities – Trash	$10–$40+		
Snow Removal	$0–$50+		
Lawn Care	$0–$150+		
	Total Monthly Budget		

Exercise: Step 2 — Preparing for Large Expenses

Tip: For home costs that do not come up each month, create a lump sum savings account. Each month, automatically transfer the monthly amount of a bill to your savings account. When your bill finally does come up, instead of having to use a credit card or borrow money, the amount you have been transferring into the automatic savings account should be enough to cover it.

Notes:
_____
_____
_____

Senior Planning Workbook

Exercise: Step 3 — Maintaining Major Home Systems (4.3)

Directions: Fill in the blanks below to calculate your projected costs.

Major Systems	Roof	Foundation Repair	Plumbing	Electrical	HVAC
Year Installed?					
How Old Is the Current System? (Current Year – Year installed)					
Estimated Lifespan	10–20 years	20–40 years	20–40 years	20–40 years	8–12 years
Years Left? (Life Span – Age of System)					
Estimated Cost	($6,000–$12,000)	($4,000–$10,000+)	($1,500–$10,000)	($2,000–$7,000)	($6,000–$10,000)
Items That May Need Replacement	Roof shingles	Foundation stabilization	Old water lines	Breaker box	Evaporator coil
Items That May Need Replacement	Decking	Outside brick	Sewer pipe	Aluminum wiring	Inside/Outside unit
Items That May Need Replacement	Water damage	Wall sheetrock	Hot water heater		Ductwork
Systems That Have Less Than Five Years Left (enter total)					
Projected Costs					

Retrofitting Your Home

Modifying a home can be expensive up front, but it can be a lot cheaper than moving into an assisted living center. In addition, staying in your home can be less burdensome than moving in with a family member.

Consult a specialist in senior home modifications. The National Association of Home Builders has a certification: *Certified Aging-In-Place Specialist*. For more info, visit *www.nahb.org*.

These specialists understand the unique needs of seniors and can make the home modifications you need. Here are some tips for when you are getting quotes and bids for making changes to your home, whether it is creating a walk-in shower, adding handrails, or whatever you need to make life a little easier.

Make sure that you are interviewing contractors who are insured and bonded — this helps to protect you in case the contractor makes a mistake on the home or breaks something.

Senior Planning Workbook

Checklist: Step 4 — Contractor Referral Check Questions (4.4)

Name: _____

Phone: _____

Email: _____

☐ When did this contractor perform work at your home?

☐ What work did this contractor do for you?

☐ How did you like the completed job?

☐ Did the contractor get the work done on budget (time and money)?

☐ Would you recommend this contractor to someone else? Why or why not?

Notes:
_____
_____
_____

Contractor Tips (4.5)

☐ Was the job completed three weeks ago or three years ago? If it is a recent referral, even better.

☐ Make sure the work you need done is something they have completed in the past. Contractors will sometimes say that they do certain work, but it is not really their specialty.

☐ If they would not recommend the contractor to somebody else, that contractor is probably not the right person for you.

☐ What happens if the work is not completed on time? You can request a penalty of $50 per day if work is not completed by a certain deadline; you can also provide an incentive for finishing early.

Notes:
_____
_____
_____

Senior Planning Workbook

Bringing in Help: Medical and Personal Care

There are two kinds of care that seniors at different stages of their lives could possibly need if they are staying in their home: Medical care and personal care.

Medical care is when a trained medical professional comes into the home and helps with medical needs, such as giving medicine or therapy.

Personal care may include taking someone to doctor's appointments, shopping, food preparation, bathing, and help with eating, dressing, or laundry.

There are many different kinds of agencies that provide these types of care. In fact, we could write a whole book on this subject. Below are some questions you can ask when interviewing a home care agency.

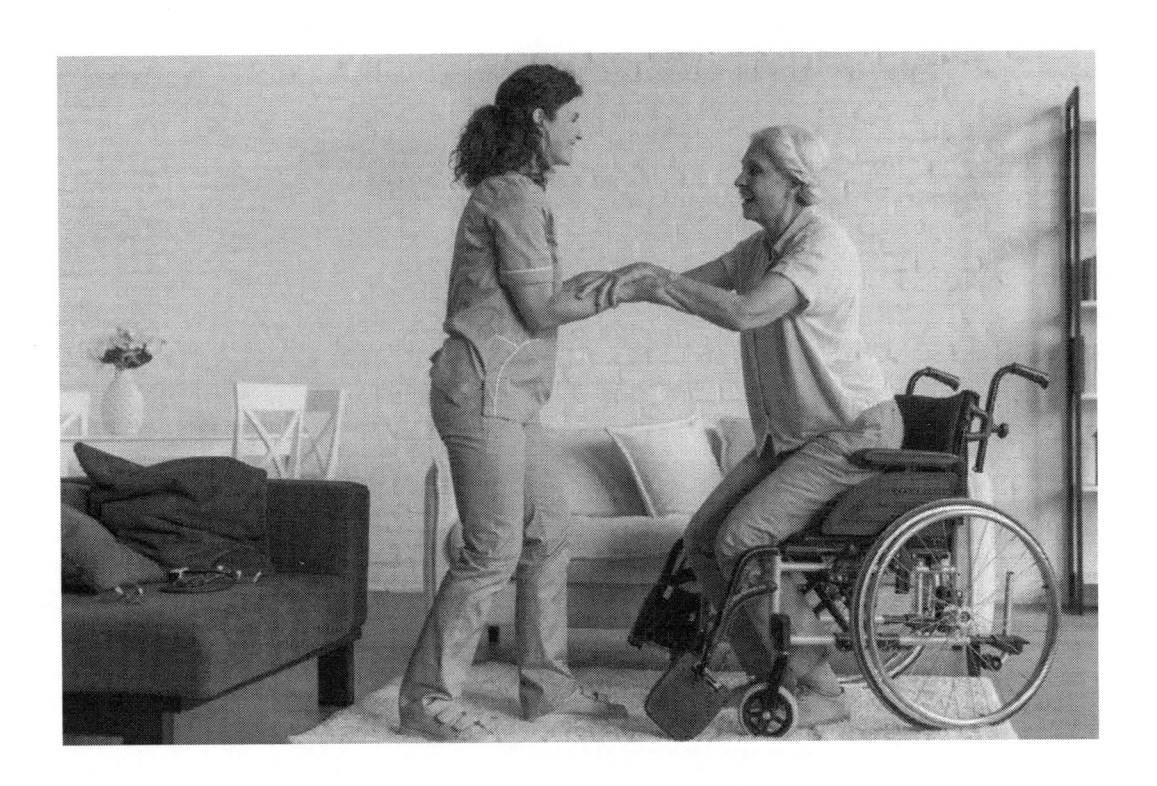

Checklist: Step 5 — Home Agency Phone Interview Questions (4.6)

Company: _____

Representative Name: _____

Phone: _____

Email: _____

☐ What services do you provide?

☐ How long have you been providing these services?

☐ Are you licensed by the state?

☐ Do you perform background checks on your staff?

☐ How will you communicate with my family members if needed?

☐ Are your caregivers available 24 hours a day?

☐ What type of fee structure do you have?

Notes:
_____
_____
_____

Chapter Summary

This chapter was written to serve the needs of those seniors who desire to continue living in their homes and have the support system in place to do so.

In this chapter, we have covered how to set your monthly home budget, prepare for large expenses, maintain your large home systems, and retrofit your home to meet any emerging mobility needs. Selecting a skilled and experienced contractor will make sure that your home receives the ideal and certified senior modifications.

Since you will be living at home and not in an assisted living facility, this chapter has also addressed the different kinds of care you will need in your home. By completing all the exercises and checklists in this chapter, you will now have a solid plan in place to keep you in your home.

For more information, reach out to us at www.kash4homes.org, 636-442-1811, or bradandchristy@theseniorhousingbook.com.

Chapter 5: Senior Housing Choices Roadmap

Chapter Goals

The goal of this chapter is to outline some of the major senior housing choices out there and list the pros and cons of each facility. New choices are becoming available all the time. What kind of facility is best for your needs right now and what types of facilities might you need in the future?

This chapter is also designed to help you better understand the cost and affordability of senior housing. The chapter contains averages across the nation and from some larger mid-priced cities, which will provide you with a starting point; then, using the tools in the previous chapter, you will be able to get the exact numbers for your area. If you go through all the exercises in this chapter, you will have a better idea of where the gaps in your current plan are and what to do next.

Three Levels of Care

1. Independent: Seniors are fully or mostly independent
2. Assisted: Personal care assistance
3. Nursing: Skilled medical care.

1. Independent Living

Age-Restricted Communities

- Age-restricted communities can be apartments, single-family homes, garden homes, and even townhouses.
- Such communities have a "connected" feeling and attract seniors who want to have access to activities ranging from arts and crafts, bingo, a gym, or a pool. Some facilities with higher-end amenities also include golf or tennis.

Pros: Ability for independent seniors to socialize with other people their own age; less home and yard maintenance than if they lived on their own.

Cons: Limited personal care and medical care services when compared to other options.

Estimated Housing Costs: $1,000–$4,000+ per month. In our customer survey, seniors were paying around $2,000 per month as a base rate and then could add optional services or memberships on top of that.

Ways to Lower the Cost: There are deals to be found in any market if you are flexible on location and amenities.

Other Things to Consider: These facilities can come retrofitted or built with mobility-restricted people in mind.

Notes:
_____
_____
_____

Senior Apartments, Townhomes, and Garden Homes

- Similar to age-restricted communities, but they usually have less amenities and are cheaper.

Pros: Great option for those who are downsizing but still want privacy. Some properties have ADA units and/or gated entrances. Such facilities are senior only.

Cons: Little or no amenities; less planned activities.

Estimated Housing Costs: $1,000–$3,000+ per month.

Ways to Lower the Cost: Friend referrals, extensive searching, and local referral agencies can help you cut the amounts above in half.

Other Things to Consider: Although the costs can be higher than a basic mortgage, they can be similar when you factor in the maintenance, other house expenses, and contractor costs required to make your existing home more livable.

Notes:

_____
_____
_____

Move-In with a Family Member

- All senior housing is more expensive than living with a family member. If something does not go according to plan or there is no plan, living with a family member may be your only option.

Pros: Integrating with your family and getting to see grandchildren on a regular basis.

Cons: If the relationship is strained or both parties are not in agreement.

Estimated Housing Costs: Free–$1,000+ per month (contribution towards expenses).

Ways to Lower the Cost: Share an apartment or small home with a sibling or adult children.

Other Things to Consider: Make sure that both parties (you and your family) agree on house rules, boundaries, privacy, etc.; address any unresolved family issues with a professional in that field before moving in.

Notes:
_____
_____
_____

Senior Planning Workbook

Renting a Room to Live In or Renting Out a Room in Your House

- You can keep your home and rent out a room. We have met people who have lived with seniors and helped them around the house in exchange for free or reduced rent.
- You do not want just anyone living in your house — it has to be the right person.

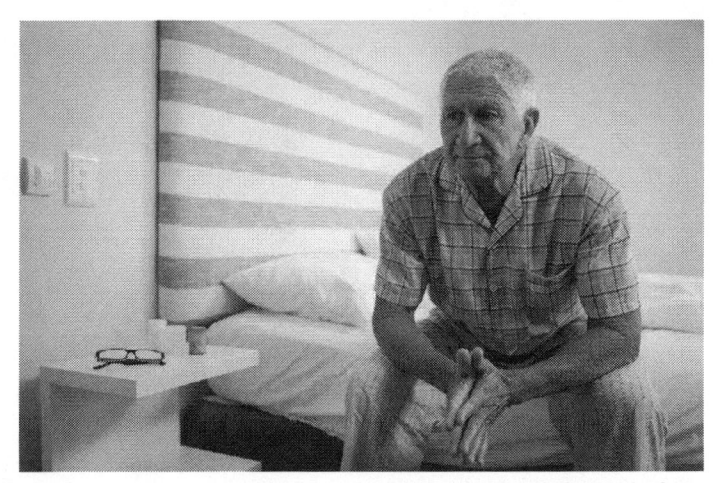

Pros: You can receive income from renting out a room or pay a reduced rate by staying with someone else.

Cons: Safety, privacy, the background of the other person, and lack of personal space and boundaries.

Estimated Housing Costs: $400–$800+ per month.

Ways to Lower the Cost: Shared room or renting out multiple rooms.

Other Things to Consider: Safety is the primary concern. If you go to live in a house with either a group of seniors or an adult that rents a room out, the same thing applies. You must be very careful anytime you live with strangers.

Notes:
_____
_____
_____

2. Assisted Living

Senior Planning Workbook

Assisted Living: Corporate Location

- Assisted living facilities can give you access to a large range of services, from help with basic personal care — such as getting dressed, taking medicine and bathing — to more advanced assistance.
- Assisted living facilities can feel like living in a big house or hotel.
- Most facilities are furnished.

Pros: Services at these facilities can include meals, daily activities, transportation, and security. Some types of memory care is available.

Cons: Most expensive option so far. Can feel impersonal.

Estimated Housing Costs: $3,000–$5,000+ per month.

Ways to Lower the Cost: Older facilities, location, and less amenities.

Other Things to Consider: Find out what services are included in the quoted rate and what services are available for an extra fee.

Notes:

_____
_____
_____

Residential Assisted Living Facilities

- These assisted living facilities are converted single-family houses in a neighborhood or small buildings that have been built to house a small group of seniors. Most facilities have between six and 18 seniors per property.

Pros: Close-knit community feel; small groups allow residents to establish close friendships; has a home feeling with the services of a larger facility; some facilities have chefs and other high-end amenities.

Cons: If you have two or three other residents that really get on your nerves, it is hard to escape from them as you could in a larger facility.

Estimated Housing Costs: $2,000–$5,500+

Ways to Lower the Cost: Shared room and less amenities

Other Things to Consider: These facilities offer some of the same services as the larger assisted living facilities but with a smaller feel.

Notes:
_____
_____
_____

Memory Care

- Memory care facilities or special care units (SCU) are specifically for patients with Alzheimer's or other forms of dementia. These units are specially designed to protect patients from getting lost. In addition, they have treatment options available to address behavioral needs, since Alzheimer's and other forms of dementia evolve with each stage.

Pros: The staff has expertise in identifying changes in stages and adjusting the patient treatment plan accordingly; patients are encouraged to live as independently as possible.

Cons: Although activities and socializing are supported at most facilities, patients can feel more closed in than non-memory care patients.

Estimated Housing Costs: $4,000–$7,000+ per month.

Ways to Lower the Cost: Ask about all-inclusive pricing versus a la carte pricing.

Other Things to Consider: The Alzheimer's Foundation of America (AFA) and The Alzheimer's Association (AA) have grant programs available for seniors who qualify.

Notes:
___
___
___

3. Nursing Care

Senior Planning Workbook

Nursing Homes

- Skilled nursing facilities (SNFs) are for individuals that require skilled nursing (medical) care. These facilities are staffed by nurses and other professionals 24 hours a day.

Pros: Services such as personal care, monitoring medical signs, management of a patient's care plan, observation of patients' conditions, and tube feedings.

Cons: Most restricted facility; services and costs vary widely.

Estimated Housing Costs: $5,500–$8,500+ per month.

Ways to Lower the Cost: Older facilities or facilities close to many other similar facilities.

Other Things to Consider: Cost is important, but make sure your senior is getting the care they need.

Notes:
_____
_____
_____

CCRC: Continuing Care Retirement Communities

- This type of community is a hybrid that can fit into all three categories.
- To be classified as a CCRC (life-plan community), a community must offer independent living, assisted living, and skilled nursing care all in the same facility or campus.
- You have to move in when you are healthy and are currently living independently.

Pros: Amenities available can be at the resort level, frequently including golf, tennis, and other higher-end amenities.

Cons: Expensive.

Estimated Housing Costs: Entry fees from low- to mid-six figures; monthly charges range from $2,000–$4,000+ per month.

Ways to Lower the Cost: Type B contracts allow you to pay for discounted care when you need it and do not require as much of a down payment.

Other Things to Consider: Communities can consist of houses, townhouses, or apartments. Type A contacts will cover all your care at the facility, even if your level of care goes up. Since the facility is taking on more risk, you are required to put down a larger down payment. If your long-term care policy will cover your extra care costs, you can elect a Type C fee for a service contract that will charge you the going rate when care is needed.

Notes:
_____
_____
_____

Chapter Summary

This chapter was written as a guide to the different senior housing options available if you are moving out of your home. We have covered the pros and cons of each, in addition to the different levels of care needs that can be accommodated.

Housing costs will vary by market and availability; however, the estimated costs shown are based on national averages, which gives you a starting point to enable you to extrapolate the numbers that would apply to you based on where you live and how the cost of living there compares to the national average.

From the information provided in this chapter, you can identify which senior housing option may work for you based on your needs and budget. In the next chapter, we will help you narrow this down even further.

For more information, reach out to us at www.kash4homes.org, 636-442-1811, or bradandchristy@theseniorhousingbook.com.

Chapter 6: Senior Housing Roadmap

Chapter Goals

If you are currently independent, figure out what will be important to you in a new facility and plan out a couple of choices from each of the categories covered in the previous chapter.

Having some facilities already narrowed down will give you and your family peace of mind in case a sudden change happens. If there has been a recent sudden change, use the information and checklists in this chapter to identify what level of care you need and start your search today.

Three Steps to Finding Your Ideal Facility

Hopefully, this framework and all the knowledge from the previous chapters will get you and your team into the right mindset to tackle this opportunity:

1. Needs and wants
2. Identify and interview
3. Decision.

Notes:

_____

_____

_____

1. Needs and Wants

You need to identify your current needs, forecast your possible future needs, and identify your wants or "wish list." Price is important, but do not let that be the sole deciding factor in your decision.

Exercise: Step 1 — Setting Up Your Plan (6.1)

Note: The following questions may be similar to the ones you answered in Chapter 2. Please answer them fully because your answers will reflect the knowledge you have gained in the chapters covered since then.

❑ Are there any current problems or challenges you are facing?

❑ What is the single biggest problem you are trying to solve?

❑ How soon do you expect to move into a senior housing facility?

❑ What geographical location do you want to live in?

❑ Do you have a specific housing need right now? If so, what is it (i.e., independent, assisted, nursing, or specialty)?

❑ What has prompted you to start this search?

❑ Where do you currently live?

❑ How long will it take to sell your home and/or move?

❑ Who are the members of your advisory team (e.g., spouse, children, family members, pastor, medical team, or professionals)?

❑ Is your advisory team part of your planning process?

Senior Planning Workbook

Exercise: Step 1 — Setting Up Your Plan Cont. (6.1)

❏ If price were no object, where would you want to live?

❏ What type of environment do you want to live in (e.g., private, community, social, private room, shared room, private house, or first floor)?

❏ What amenities would you like to have available (e.g., entertainment, recreation, food, pool, classes, and transportation)?

❏ What types of personal care services do you need now or want to be available (e.g., dressing, mobility help, laundry, bathing, and food)?

❏ What type of medical care services do you need now or want to be available (e.g., treatments, specialty care, medicine, or diabetes care)?

Notes:

_____
_____
_____

Exercise: Step 2 — Your Team (6.2)

Directions: List Your Professional Team and Contact Info	
Professional	**Contact Info**
Attorney:	
Financial Advisor:	
CPA:	
Medical Team:	
Medical Team:	
Other Advisor:	
Other Advisor:	

❏ Let us review your advisory team list from Chapter 2. Have there been any changes? If so, what are they?

❏ Are there any other needs or wants you have not mentioned yet that are important to you?

❏ What is important to the members of your advisory team? Ask them if you have not already, e.g., "I am creating a Senior Housing Plan that I expect to begin following (fill in the date, for example, next month, next year, or ten years). What is important to you?

❏ Ask your advisory team, "Is there anything else you want me to consider as I am creating my plan?"

Notes:

_____

_____

_____

Senior Planning Workbook

Checklist: Step 3 — Closest Advisor Questions (6.3)

❏ Do you have any concerns regarding my health, safety, or overall happiness?

❏ What problems or challenges are you facing as my top advisor?

❏ Is moving in with you or anyone else in our family an option?

Notes:

_____
_____
_____

Exercise: Step 4 — Your Budget (6.4)

(**Note:** Some of these are a recap of what you may have answered in preceding chapters).

❑ Do you use a monthly budget?

❑ What monthly amount can you afford for senior housing and care expenses?

❑ What financial sources are available to pay for senior housing?

❑ If you do not need senior housing right now, have you inquired about long-term care insurance?

❑ Do you expect family members to help pay for your housing? If so, how much do they plan to contribute?

❑ If you plan to sell your home, how much do you expect to receive?

Notes:
_____
_____
_____

Exercise: Step 5 — Other Planning Questions (6.5)

❏ Are you married?

❏ Do you currently live with anyone else?

❏ If you move, where is your current house partner (e.g., friend, family, or spouse) going to live?

❏ If your spouse were to die before you, would you want to stay in your current home?

❏ Would you prefer to move into a facility that has all the care options available, from independent to nursing, or would you be fine moving to a new facility if you needed more care?

❏ Do you want to be close to a church or place of worship? Which one?

❏ Is there a friend or family member you want to live close to?

❏ If you are thinking about moving across the city, state, or country, will you need to find a new doctor or other professionals?

❏ If you are moving into a furnished facility, what is the plan for your current furniture and personal belongings?

Home To Home

Exercise: Step 5 — Other Planning Questions Cont. (6.5)

❏ If you plan to give items from your home away to family members, have you let your family members know?

❏ Will you get input from your family members before giving them any of your personal belongings?

❏ When you give a family member or friend your personal belongings, are the items theirs to keep or are you just letting them store them for you?

❏ Will you need to rent a storage facility? If so, where?

❏ How will you know when it is time to make a decision?

Notes:
_____
_____
_____

Senior Planning Workbook

2. Identify and Interview

Once you map out what is important to you and your team and you have a basic budget idea of what you want and need, start identifying and interviewing facilities. You can find facilities online, from print media, referrals from friends, or by contacting local or national referral services.

Answer the following questions at each step of the process. After narrowing down your choices, you should plan to visit a minimum of three to four facilities of each type of care for which you are planning. Carry a checklist for each facility so that you can evaluate and compare them at the end.

Exercise: Step 6 — Before You Call Questions (Identify) (6.6)

Directions: Circle housing type and fill out contact information		
Independent	**Assisted**	**Nursing**
Age-Restricted Community	Assisted Living – Corp.	Nursing Home
Senior Apartments	Residential Assisted Living	CCRC
Senior Townhomes	Memory Care	Other
Senior Garden Homes	Other	
Live with Family		
Rent or Rent Out Room		
Other		
Facility Name:		
Phone Number:		
Address:		
Website:	Email:	

❏ How did I find out about this facility?

❏ How many of my needs does this facility meet?

❏ How many of my wants does this facility meet?

❏ Does this facility have the level of care I may need in the future?

❏ What do the online reviews say about this facility (see Google, Facebook, and the Better Business Bureau)?

Checklist: Step 7 — Call the Facility (Phone Interview) (6.7)

Directions: Fill out contact information and answers to all questions	
Facility:	Phone #:
Talked to:	Date/Time:

❏ Do you have any openings at your facility?

❏ What services do you provide?

❏ Do you perform background checks on your staff? What about the residents?

❏ Is your facility accredited? If so, with whom?

❏ How much should I budget for if I move into your facility (not an exact number, just a range)?

❏ If I become a resident, how often do rates change?

❏ What is the best way that I can get more information about your facility?

❏ When can I take a tour of the facility and learn more?

Checklist: Step 8 — Tour Questions (In Person Interview) (6.8)

Directions: Fill out contact information and answers to all questions	
Facility:	Phone #:
Address:	
Talked to:	Date and Time:

❑ Ask your tour person how long they have worked there and what their main focus is.

❑ Who is the current manager or director? How long have they been there?

❑ What services are not offered here?

❑ What do you like about working here?

❑ What would you change about the facility if you could?

❑ Ask if you can speak to any other employees and residents about their experience at the facility.

❑ How do you communicate with family members?

❑ What are their visiting hours?

Checklist: Step 8 — Tour Questions (In Person Interview) Cont. (6.8)

❏ Do they have any referrals of current residents or past residents/family members you can contact?

❏ Is this a for profit or non-profit facility? If you have experience with each one, what differences do you see in this one?

❏ If I were to move in today and order certain services, what would my price be?

❏ How often do rates change?

❏ How many openings do you have right now?

❏ Is the rate open to negotiation? If so, under what circumstances?

❏ What is the application process? How long does it take?

❏ Are there any questions I should have asked that I did not?

❏ How long can we take to make a decision?

3. Decision

After your interviews and tours, it is time to sit down with your team and narrow the list down to your top two choices. If you need to move quickly, call your top facility and start the application process. If your top facility is not available when you need it, you can choose the alternative.

On the next page is a comparison chart you can fill out together with your advisory team.

Senior Planning Workbook

Checklist: Step 9 — Facility Comparison Part 1 (6.9)

Directions: You invested time in researching, calling, and visiting different facilities — now it is time to rank your top two choices. Since different things are important to different people, you are going to customize your comparison checklist to what is most important to you.

Tip: Try to focus on the questions and not the answers received in Part 1 of this exercise.

Step 1: Review all the questions in the *Before You Call Checklist*.

What is the number one most important question to YOU on that checklist? Circle it.

Step 2: Review the questions on the *Call The Facility Checklist*.

What are the top two most important questions to YOU on that checklist? Circle them.

Step 3: Review the questions on the *Tour Questions Checklist*.

What are the top three most important questions to YOU on that checklist? Circle them.

Notes:
_____
_____
_____

Checklist: Step 10 — Facility Comparison Part 2 (6.10)

Directions: Write the names of your top two facilities. Write your top question(s) for each checklist on the left side of the table. Give each answer a score and total up each facility. Use the scoring guide at the bottom.

Facility Name (Top Two)		
Score	1–10	1–10
Before You Call Questions:		
Call the Facility Questions:		
Call the Facility Questions:		
Tour Questions:		
Tour Questions:		
Tour Questions:		
Total (total your six scores)		
Score: 60–48 = Great 47–42 = Average 41 and Below = No	Great Average No	Great Average No

Next Steps: Tips

- ❏ If you need to move quickly, call your top facility and start the application process. If your top facility is not available when you need it, you can choose the alternative.

- ❏ If your preferred facility is full but you are not in an immediate rush, make sure to get added to the waiting list. If you are still planning, you can get on the waiting list **AHEAD** of time.

- ❏ If your facility has high demand, consider putting a deposit down to hold your spot while you go through the application process.

- ❏ Can you afford the place you have selected? If not, it is better to check it off the list now instead of living there for a short period of time and then having to move because of a lack of finances. Go back to the financial section of the workbook and talk the numbers over with your team.

- ❏ Make sure you understand all the costs involved and get them in writing so that there is no confusion later.

- ❏ You can negotiate the rates at some facilities. We have had customers who have received move-in specials and some services added at a discount. Keep in mind that there are many things more important than price — do you want to be in a facility that serves bad food and has very low energy simply to save $500 a month?

- ❏ If moving into a senior housing facility is not in the immediate future, having a couple of choices in each of the three areas narrowed down will drastically cut down on the time it takes to pick the search back up when the timeline becomes more immediate.

❏ If your budget is on the lower side, you will want to start planning even sooner because great places at budget prices fill up faster in most markets.

❏ Look for a place that has a good value-to-cost ratio. You may not get everything on your wish list, so be willing to make compromises if you have to on the items that are not as important to you.

❏ If you have long-term care insurance and a significant nest egg saved up, pick your dream location. Enjoy your senior housing experience!

Reach Out to Us for Help

We would love to assist you in any way possible — we are here to help!

For more information, reach out to us at www.kash4homes.org, 636-442-1811, or bradandchristy@theseniorhousingbook.com.

Chapter Summary

This chapter was written to help you take stock of your current needs and wants, identify potential facilities and conduct interviews with their staff, and score your top two facilities of choice based on your most important questions.

Knowing that price is not the only thing to keep in mind, by now you will have a laser focus on your facility of choice and an alternative if your preferred option is not available.

Chapter 7: Paying For Senior Housing

Chapter Goals

Now that you know the types of housing options and some of the costs, this chapter will focus on some of the different ways to pay for senior housing. Please consult your financial advisor, attorney, and advisory team to fill in all the details.

Medicare

Pays For:

- ☐ Medical costs
- ☐ Medical care at skilled nursing homes
- ☐ Some types of medical care at assisted living facilities if they are administered by an independent third party or at home
- ☐ If you qualify, a 20-day-or-less stay in a skilled nursing facility (after 20 days, you have to pay for part of the costs until the 100th day).

Does Not Pay For:

- ☐ The cost of *staying* in any long-term facility
- ☐ Personal care
- ☐ Eating
- ☐ Transportation
- ☐ Bathing
- ☐ Other personal care items that are considered non-medical
- ☐ Skilled nursing care after 100 days.

Medicare Supplemental Insurance

Pays For:

☐ Gaps from day 20 to 100 in a skilled nursing home facility.

Does Not Pay For

☐ Care that lasts over 100 days.

Medicaid

Medicaid is for low-income individuals that have very limited financial assets. If you qualify, Medicaid…

Pays For:

☐ Nursing care (medical and non-medical expenses) and some home care expenses.

Does Not Pay For:

☐ Assisted living (there are very few assisted living locations available for people on Medicaid. If you only need assisted living care and have very limited financial means, you are probably not going to find a place).

Long-Term Care Insurance

Depending on the policy, long-term care insurance starts kicking in when a senior cannot perform two of the six activities of daily living (ADLs):

- ☐ Eating
- ☐ Going to the bathroom
- ☐ Getting out of a bed or chair
- ☐ Walking
- ☐ Dressing
- ☐ Bathing.

Once activated…

Pays For:

- ☐ Assisted living
- ☐ Nursing care
- ☐ Alzheimer's facilities
- ☐ Home modification
- ☐ Home care
- ☐ Adult day care
- ☐ Hospice care and more
- ☐ Sometimes, a live-in caregiver.

Reverse Mortgage

Instead of taking out a mortgage yourself and making payments to buy a house, a reverse mortgage company will put a lien on a high-equity or paid-off house and then pay you.

Pros

- ☐ A way for you to take equity out of your house without having to sell it.
- ☐ If you can keep paying the taxes, insurance, and maintenance for your home, you can stay in it until you pass away or move.
- ☐ The money that you use from the reverse mortgage will be used during your life and will reduce the amount of your estate.

Cons

- ☐ Can be foreclosed on under certain circumstances.
- ☐ Customers have to remember to keep paying their insurance and annual property taxes.
- ☐ The fine print of some contracts state that not keeping up the maintenance on your home will be considered a default against your reverse mortgage, and the lender can foreclose.
- ☐ On some reverse mortgage agreements, if one of the homeowners dies, the spouse is required to pay back a large amount or the full amount of the loan.
- ☐ Interest rates can be high.

Other Ways to Pay

- ☐ Private pay
- ☐ Veteran programs for assisted living (aid and attendance benefit)
- ☐ Veterans direct care
- ☐ State non-Medicaid programs
- ☐ Medicaid home and community-based service waivers
- ☐ Medicaid 1915 waivers
- ☐ Life insurance options (benefits before death)
- ☐ Assisted living loans.

Other Resources

- ☐ Financial advisor
- ☐ Attorney
- ☐ Members of your advisory team
- ☐ Area agencies on aging counselors
- ☐ Aging and disability resource center counselors
- ☐ Geriatric care managers
- ☐ Eldercare resource planners.

Things to Watch Out for

- ☐ Prices going up for senior housing
- ☐ Rates increasing each year while you are in senior housing
- ☐ Fine print
- ☐ Understanding the base price and any additional costs
- ☐ What Medicare will and will not pay for
- ☐ What the qualifications are for Medicaid.

Reach Out to Us

Our specialty is housing. If you need a referral for someone to help you with the financial part of your plan, give us a call and we will refer you to someone we know, like, and trust. For more information, reach out to us at www.kash4homes.org, 636-442-1811, or bradandchristy@theseniorhousingbook.com.

Chapter Summary

The goal of this chapter has been to give you some information on the costs of senior housing and the different ways to pay for it. Senior housing can be a significant expense.

The next chapter will address some special challenges family members have with the senior planning process. We hope that the chapter and the questions therein will help your family get more clarity.

Chapter 8: Special Challenges For Family Members Of Seniors

Chapter Goals

Some of the most overlooked and misunderstood people in the senior housing process are the family members who take care of seniors, particularly those with significant health, mental, or mobility problems. The goal of this chapter is to shine a light on family members who have dedicated themselves to attending the needs of their senior loved ones.

According to Rich Johnson at the Urban Institute, about 10% of Americans over the age of 65 have long-term care insurance.[1]

How are the other 90% of seniors going to pay for senior housing, and what kind of impact will this have on their families?

In the following pages, you will read about the struggles seniors' family members face and some recommendations on how to handle them. The questions in this and previous chapters are not a replacement for consulting professional counselors, advisors, and attorneys, but they are a great starting point for getting some concerns out in the open so that you can come up with a plan to resolve them.

The questions, concerns, and challenges listed below have been sent in by our senior customers' family members, and we hope these concerns and recommendations give your family clarity.

---

[1] Source: Gleckman, H. "Who Owns Long-Term Care Insurance?" *Forbes Magazine*, 18 August 2016. Retrieved from www.forbes.com/sites/howardgleckman/2016/08/18/who-owns-long-term-care-insurance/#121f9d6f2f05

Lack of Appreciation from Seniors Being Taken Care of by Family Members

Think back to when you were kids and your parents spent two hours preparing dinner. They would spend time slaving away on a gourmet meal, and how did you show your appreciation?

"No thanks, I want something else!"

Maybe you were the exception, but parents hear that all the time. It is hard to not take it personally when you are not appreciated.

Are you going to be appreciated all the time when you are taking care of a senior family member? It depends. Even if your senior has a great disposition, it can be tough when they are sick or in pain.

It is fine to tell your family member how you feel, but sometimes there is not much of a change. Be patient and find another family member or friend you can confide in.

Strained Relationships Before Care Began

If your relationship with your senior is strained before they get sick or need your help, it is probably not going to get any better when more emotional, financial, and physical stress gets piled on top.

We are huge fans of counseling. The more you can include a trained third-party advisor in helping you, the better. Counseling can come from a trained family member, a church leader, or a private counselor. Most strained relationships did not get that way overnight, so do not expect the tension to dissipate immediately. However, you can start making progress today.

Caring for Seniors with Memory Issues

Your mood and energy is going to rub off on your senior. If you are positive and happy, this will encourage them and give you more patience. Speak to your senior in simple sentences that involve 'yes' or 'no' answers. If your senior does not answer right away, be patient.

If you need your senior to do something that involves many steps, start with Step 1 and do not talk about Step 2 until Step 1 is complete. If your senior gets mad at you, talk about something else or go for a walk; maybe get something to eat. The change in scenery can help redirect the issue.

Sometimes, going through old photos can be a fun activity. Many seniors with memory issues cannot remember what you told them 30 minutes ago, but they can remember what was going on in a photo 30 years before.[2]

Major Health Issues

According to a recent survey by the AARP Public Policy Institute and National Alliance for Caregiving, one in three people caring for someone at home hired paid help to assist them in the home.

If you are caring for a senior at home, start planning to get extra help, even if you do not need it right now. If your senior is over 55 and certified by the state as in need of nursing home-level care, see if the area you live in offers a PACE program, which is for people on Medicare or Medicaid and covers in-home care, doctor care, and transportation. For more details, be sure to visit *https://www.medicare.gov/your-medicare-costs/get-help-paying-costs/pace*.[3]

Financial Issues

Hopefully, you got this book early in the process, and so you now understand the enormous costs involved in senior care and can start working backwards to figure out what you are going to do.

Lack of communication contributes significantly to this stress factor. Many of the families we work with do not talk about money until they have to. Look into local programs for seniors offered by religious institutions and not-for-profit organizations like United Way.[4]

---

[2] Source: "6 Best Ways to Stimulate Memories through Photos," *Alzheimers.net*, 6 October 2014. Retrieved from www.alzheimers.net/10-6-14-memories-photos/
[3] Source: "PACE," *Medicare*. Retrieved from www.medicare.gov/your-medicare-costs/get-help-paying-costs/pace
[4] Source: "Aging," *United Way Worldwide*. Retrieved from www.unitedway.org/our-impact/featured-programs/aging

One Sibling Doing All the Work or Blocking Other People from Seeing the Senior

The sooner you start mapping out the role and contribution of everyone on the advisory team, the sooner you will get clarity on what the next steps are. If you are the sibling doing all the work taking care of your senior, let the other family members know that you need their help and ask them what they are willing or able to do. Do not assume anything.

If there is a gatekeeper involved blocking you out, attempt to visit and help out. If that does not work, you can still send your senior letters and emails to let them know that you care about them.

Taking Care of Senior Parents while Still Taking Care of Children at Home

Questions to Consider:

☐ Will you be able to financially support your family and your parents at the same time? If not, who can you involve to help?

☐ Is there physically enough room in your house for your family and your parents to live?

☐ Do you have the option of moving to a larger home or adding on to your existing home?

☐ How will your senior parents integrate with your children?

☐ What will you do if there are disagreements?

☐ How will you manage your time so that you can be with your spouse, children, and parents and still have time for yourself?

☐ How will you modify your schedule?

Feeling Guilty for Putting Your Parents in Senior Living Facilities

Questions to Consider:

☐ What is best for your senior?

☐ Are you doing everything you can to make sure they are in the best facility possible?

☐ How can you still be involved with your senior and make them feel loved while they are living in a senior housing facility?

Each Adult Child Sibling Sees the Senior's Needs Differently

Questions to Consider:

☐ Who is the primary decision maker for the senior?

☐ Does everyone know who the primary decision maker is?

☐ Are all the adult children part of the planning process?

☐ Did you include the concerns of all the adult children before you started putting your plan together?

The Senior Does Not Want to Admit That They Need Help

Questions to Consider:

☐ Have you explained your concerns to your senior?

☐ Have other children and family members expressed their concerns for the senior?

☐ Are your concerns being presented as bossy or caring?

☐ Have you asked your senior why they do not feel the same way you do?

☐ Is your senior still of sound mind?

☐ If not, have you contacted your attorney to investigate the guardianship process?

How to Pay for Senior Care

Questions to Consider:

☐ Are all family members involved in contributing to senior costs?

☐ Is one family member the main decision maker for financial matters?

☐ Have you consulted your financial advisor for advice?

☐ Have you contacted local churches and non-profits regarding free or reduced services for seniors?

☐ Does your senior qualify for government or veteran benefits?

Caring for Both Parents at Once

Questions To Consider:

☐ Do you have enough financial, emotional, and physical strength to take care of both parents?

☐ What are the different needs of each parent?

☐ Can another family member move in or stop by regularly to help you take care of both parents?

In Closing

We hope you have received a great deal of value from this workbook — even one tip can make a huge difference in your senior's outcomes. God bless you and your family during your senior housing journey. We will keep you all in our prayers.

For more information, reach out to us at www.kash4homes.org, 636-442-1811, or bradandchristy@theseniorhousingbook.com.

Appendix

What Is Included in This Section

Our goal for this workbook has been for you to keep all the documents you fill out so that they cannot get lost, which is why we do not offer downloadable checklists and worksheets.

If you fill everything out inside this book, you will be able to find it when you need it. Copies of the exercises and multiple copies of the checklists can be found in the following pages so that if you make a mistake on a checklist or an exercise, you can just go on to the next one. The multiple copies are marked (1.1, 1.2, 3.1, 3.3, etc.) so as to make them easy to track.

Instead of tearing them out, fill them out directly in the Appendix; in that way, they will always be close at hand when you need them.

Enjoy!

Senior Planning Workbook

Contact Information (1.1)

Directions: Fill out the contact information below.

Senior Name: _____

Senior's Spouse's Name: _____

Address: _____

Phone: _____

Email: _____

Today's Date: _____

Emergency Contacts

Contact #1

Name: _____

Relation: _____

Phone Number: _____

Alternative Phone Number: _____

Email Address: _____

Contact #2

Name: _____

Relation: _____

Phone Number: _____

Alternative Phone Number: _____

Email Address: _____

Advisory Team (1.2)

Directions: List Your Professional Team and Contact Info	
Professional	**Contact Info**
Attorney:	
Financial Advisor:	
CPA:	
Medical Team:	
Medical Team:	
Other Advisor:	
Other Advisor:	

Closest Advisor: This could be the executor of your will or estate, a close family member, or another member of your advisory team. Choose this person carefully. Make sure that this person will execute your wishes and is looking out for your best interests. If there is no one in your family that would fit this role, an attorney can (if established ahead of time).

Notes:
_____
_____
_____

Senior Planning Workbook

Banking (1.3)

Banking and Investment Information			
Type	Company Name	Account Number	Phone Number
Checking			
Checking			
Savings			
Savings			
Investment			
Investment			
Other			
Other			
Other			
Other			

Homework: Print out all the statements from each of these accounts and put them in the same safe and secure place you will be keeping your workbook.

Real Estate (1.4)

Primary Residence	
Property Address	
Paid Off?	(Circle One) YES NO
Name of Title Holder(s)	
Mortgage Company Information	
Company Name	
Phone Number	
Account Number	
2nd Mortgage (on Same Property)	
Company Name	
Phone Number	
Account Number	

Other Property	
Property Address	
Property Paid Off?	(Circle One) YES NO
Name of Title Holder(s)	
Mortgage Company Information	
Company Name	
Phone Number	
Account Number	
2nd Mortgage (on Same Property)	
Company Name	
Phone Number	
Account Number	

Homework: Print out all the statements from each of these accounts and put them in the same safe and secure place you will be keeping your workbook.

Insurance (1.5)

Insurance Provider Information			
Type	**Company Name**	**Policy Number**	**Phone Number**
Health			
Life			
Disability			
Long-Term Care			
Homeowner's			
Auto			
Other			
Other			

Homework: Print out each of these policies and put them in the same safe and secure place you will be keeping your workbook.

Notes:
_____
_____
_____

Legal (1.6)

Legal Document Information		
Document Type	**Have You Created This Document? (Yes or No)**	**Date Created**
Medical Directive		
Durable Power of Attorney for Healthcare and HIPAA Release		
Durable Power of Attorney for Finances		
Revocable Living Trust		
Will		

Homework: Make a copy of all these documents and keep them in your secure location.

Notes:
___
___

Senior Planning Workbook

Computer Passwords (1.7)

Tip: For added security, look into getting an online password vault that will store all your passwords for you — our company uses *1Password*. You will be able to save all your passwords and create vaults for your family members so that you can give them access to your accounts if needed.

Website	User Name	Password

Home To Home

Exercise: Monthly Budget (2.1)

Directions: Fill out this sample budget using your current income and expenses and then total up each section. When each section has been totaled, subtract the total of each expense section from your total income — this will show you your monthly surplus (extra) or deficit (shortfall).

Income	Monthly	Medical Expenses	Monthly
Wages from Employment		Health Insurance	
Social Security		Regular Prescriptions	
401K or IRA Income		Out-of-Pocket	
Pension Benefit		**Medical Total**	
Rental Property Income			
Other		**Personal Expenses**	**Monthly**
Income Total		Clothing	
		Toiletries	
Housing Expenses	**Monthly**	Miscellaneous	
Rent/Mortgage/Taxes		Movies/Books	
Maintenance/Lawn		Cable TV	
Electric/Gas		Travel	
Water/Sewer/Garbage		**Personal Total**	
Phone/Internet			
Housing Total		**Debt**	**Monthly**
		Credit Card Payments	
Food/Car Expenses	**Monthly**	Personal Loan Payments	
Groceries		**Debt Total**	
Restaurants			
Car Payment/Insurance		**Total Monthly Income**	
Gasoline		**Total Monthly Expenses**	
Car Repairs		**Deficit or Surplus**	
Other			
Food/Car Total			

111

Senior Planning Workbook

Exercise: Monthly Budget (2.1)

Directions: Fill out this sample budget using your current income and expenses and then total up each section. When each section has been totaled, subtract the total of each expense section from your total income — this will show you your monthly surplus (extra) or deficit (shortfall).

Income	Monthly	Medical Expenses	Monthly
Wages from Employment		Health Insurance	
Social Security		Regular Prescriptions	
401K or IRA Income		Out-of-Pocket	
Pension Benefit		**Medical Total**	
Rental Property Income			
Other		**Personal Expenses**	**Monthly**
Income Total		Clothing	
		Toiletries	
Housing Expenses	**Monthly**	Miscellaneous	
Rent/Mortgage/Taxes		Movies/Books	
Maintenance/Lawn		Cable TV	
Electric/Gas		Travel	
Water/Sewer/Garbage		**Personal Total**	
Phone/Internet			
Housing Total		**Debt**	**Monthly**
		Credit Card Payments	
Food/Car Expenses	**Monthly**	Personal Loan Payments	
Groceries		**Debt Total**	
Restaurants			
Car Payment/Insurance		**Total Monthly Income**	
Gasoline		**Total Monthly Expenses**	
Car Repairs		**Deficit or Surplus**	
Other			
Food/Car Total			

Exercise: Monthly Budget (2.1)

Directions: Fill out this sample budget using your current income and expenses and then total up each section. When each section has been totaled, subtract the total of each expense section from your total income — this will show you your monthly surplus (extra) or deficit (shortfall).

Income	Monthly	Medical Expenses	Monthly
Wages from Employment		Health Insurance	
Social Security		Regular Prescriptions	
401K or IRA Income		Out-of-Pocket	
Pension Benefit		**Medical Total**	
Rental Property Income			
Other		**Personal Expenses**	**Monthly**
Income Total		Clothing	
		Toiletries	
Housing Expenses	**Monthly**	Miscellaneous	
Rent/Mortgage/Taxes		Movies/Books	
Maintenance/Lawn		Cable TV	
Electric/Gas		Travel	
Water/Sewer/Garbage		**Personal Total**	
Phone/Internet			
Housing Total		**Debt**	**Monthly**
		Credit Card Payments	
Food/Car Expenses	**Monthly**	Personal Loan Payments	
Groceries		**Debt Total**	
Restaurants			
Car Payment/Insurance		**Total Monthly Income**	
Gasoline		**Total Monthly Expenses**	
Car Repairs		**Deficit or Surplus**	
Other			
Food/Car Total			

Exercise: Home Condition (3.1)

When was the last time your home was remodeled or updated?

(This can help you figure out the value of your home).

Date Updated	Updates Made	Amount Spent

Exercise: Home Inventory (3.2)

If you sell your home, what items do you plan to bring with you to your new home or apartment?

(Take a few minutes to think about the items in your home and what your plans for them are).

Item Description	Keep or Pass On?	If Pass On, To Whom?

Exercise: Home Inventory (3.2)

If you sell your home, what items do you plan to bring with you to your new home or apartment?

(Take a few minutes to think about the items in your home and what your plans for them are).

Item Description	Keep or Pass On?	If Pass On, To Whom?

Real Estate Agent Questions (3.3)

(Before You Call)

☐ Is your home updated to current standards? YES   NO

☐ Does your home need any repairs?   YES   NO

(If yes, fill out the table below).

Part of the Home	Repairs Needed	Estimated Price

☐ When do you need to sell your home by?

☐ How long will you need to move out of your home and take care of your possessions?

☐ If your home sells faster than your new home is ready, who would you stay with or where would you move to temporarily (less than 30 days).

Senior Planning Workbook

Real Estate Agent Questions (3.3)

(Before You Call)

☐ Is your home updated to current standards? YES   NO

☐ Does your home need any repairs?   YES   NO

(If yes, fill out the table below).

Part of the Home	Repairs Needed	Estimated Price

☐ When do you need to sell your home by?

☐ How long will you need to move out of your home and take care of your possessions?

☐ If your home sells faster than your new home is ready, who would you stay with or where would you move to temporarily (less than 30 days).

Real Estate Agent Questions (3.3)

(Before You Call)

☐ Is your home updated to current standards? YES   NO

☐ Does your home need any repairs?   YES   NO

(If yes, fill out the table below).

Part of the Home	Repairs Needed	Estimated Price

☐ When do you need to sell your home by?

☐ How long will you need to move out of your home and take care of your possessions?

☐ If your home sells faster than your new home is ready, who would you stay with or where would you move to temporarily (less than 30 days).

Senior Planning Workbook

Real Estate Agent Questions (3.3)

(Before You Call)

☐ Is your home updated to current standards? YES   NO

☐ Does your home need any repairs?   YES   NO

(If yes, fill out the table below).

Part of the Home	Repairs Needed	Estimated Price

☐ When do you need to sell your home by?

☐ How long will you need to move out of your home and take care of your possessions?

☐ If your home sells faster than your new home is ready, who would you stay with or where would you move to temporarily (less than 30 days).

Real Estate Agent Questions (3.3)

(Before You Call)

☐ Is your home updated to current standards? YES   NO

☐ Does your home need any repairs?   YES   NO

(If yes, fill out the table below).

Part of the Home	Repairs Needed	Estimated Price

☐ When do you need to sell your home by?

☐ How long will you need to move out of your home and take care of your possessions?

☐ If your home sells faster than your new home is ready, who would you stay with or where would you move to temporarily (less than 30 days).

Senior Planning Workbook

Real Estate Agent Questions (3.4)

(In Person)

☐ How long have you been in business?

☐ Are you full time or part time?

☐ Is the real estate agent you are considering related to you? If yes, how would a negative real estate transaction impact on your family relationships?

☐ What neighborhood do you specialize in?

☐ Have you helped buy or sell a house in this neighborhood in the last 12 months?

☐ How much is my house worth in its current condition? How did you come up with that number?

☐ Based on the market and this neighborhood, how long will it take to sell my home?

☐ When we get an offer, what types of repairs, closing cost contributions, or price reductions are possible?

☐ Can I contact your **references**?

Home To Home

Real Estate Agent Questions (3.4)

(In Person)

☐ How long have you been in business?

☐ Are you full time or part time?

☐ Is the real estate agent you are considering related to you? If yes, how would a negative real estate transaction impact on your family relationships?

☐ What neighborhood do you specialize in?

☐ Have you helped buy or sell a house in this neighborhood in the last 12 months?

☐ How much is my house worth in its current condition? How did you come up with that number?

☐ Based on the market and this neighborhood, how long will it take to sell my home?

☐ When we get an offer, what types of repairs, closing cost contributions, or price reductions are possible?

☐ Can I contact your **references**?

Senior Planning Workbook

Real Estate Agent Questions (3.4)

(In Person)

☐ How long have you been in business?

☐ Are you full time or part time?

☐ Is the real estate agent you are considering related to you? If yes, how would a negative real estate transaction impact on your family relationships?

☐ What neighborhood do you specialize in?

☐ Have you helped buy or sell a house in this neighborhood in the last 12 months?

☐ How much is my house worth in its current condition? How did you come up with that number?

☐ Based on the market and this neighborhood, how long will it take to sell my home?

☐ When we get an offer, what types of repairs, closing cost contributions, or price reductions are possible?

☐ Can I contact your **references**?

Real Estate Agent Questions (3.4)

(In Person)

☐ How long have you been in business?

☐ Are you full time or part time?

☐ Is the real estate agent you are considering related to you? If yes, how would a negative real estate transaction impact on your family relationships?

☐ What neighborhood do you specialize in?

☐ Have you helped buy or sell a house in this neighborhood in the last 12 months?

☐ How much is my house worth in its current condition? How did you come up with that number?

☐ Based on the market and this neighborhood, how long will it take to sell my home?

☐ When we get an offer, what types of repairs, closing cost contributions, or price reductions are possible?

☐ Can I contact your **references**?

Senior Planning Workbook

Real Estate Agent Questions (3.4)

(In Person)

☐ How long have you been in business?

☐ Are you full time or part time?

☐ Is the real estate agent you are considering related to you? If yes, how would a negative real estate transaction impact on your family relationships?

☐ What neighborhood do you specialize in?

☐ Have you helped buy or sell a house in this neighborhood in the last 12 months?

☐ How much is my house worth in its current condition? How did you come up with that number?

☐ Based on the market and this neighborhood, how long will it take to sell my home?

☐ When we get an offer, what types of repairs, closing cost contributions, or price reductions are possible?

☐ Can I contact your **references**?

Home To Home

Project Planning (3.5)

(Before You Do the Work)

☐ How much money are you willing to invest in updating your home before selling it?

☐ How will you pay for remodeling your home?

(Circle any that apply)

Cash	Credit Card	Reverse Mortgage	Home Equity Line of Credit
Family Loan	Bank Loan	Other	Home Equity Mortgage

☐ What updates would your home need to be up to current remodeling standards?

Part of the Home	Update Needed	Estimated Price

☐ How soon do you need to get the repairs completed?

☐ Do you need a contractor referral? If yes, you can call our office at 636-442-1811 for a referral or if you have any questions you need answered.

Senior Planning Workbook

Project Planning (3.5)

(Before You Do the Work)

☐ How much money are you willing to invest in updating your home before selling it?

☐ How will you pay for remodeling your home?

(Circle any that apply)

Cash	Credit Card	Reverse Mortgage	Home Equity Line of Credit
Family Loan	Bank Loan	Other	Home Equity Mortgage

☐ What updates would your home need to be up to current remodeling standards?

Part of the Home	Update Needed	Estimated Price

☐ How soon do you need to get the repairs completed?

☐ Do you need a contractor referral? If yes, you can call our office at 636-442-1811 for a referral or if you have any questions you need answered.

Contractor Questions (3.6)

(Before You Do the Work)

Directions: Fill this out before you meet the contractor.

Company: _____

Representative Name: _____

Phone: _____

Email: _____

❏ How did you find out about this contractor?

❏ What services does this contractor offer?

❏ Is the contractor insured and bonded?

❏ Does the contractor have any specialties?

❏ What do the online reviews say about this contractor (see Google, Facebook, and the Better Business Bureau)?

Notes:

_____
_____
_____

Contractor Questions (3.6)

(Before You Do the Work)

Directions: Fill this out before you meet the contractor.

Company: _____

Representative Name: _____

Phone: _____

Email: _____

❏ How did you find out about this contractor?

❏ What services does this contractor offer?

❏ Is the contractor insured and bonded?

❏ Does the contractor have any specialties?

❏ What do the online reviews say about this contractor (see Google, Facebook, and the Better Business Bureau)?

Notes:
_____
_____
_____

Home To Home

Contractor Questions (3.6)

(Before You Do the Work)

Directions: Fill this out before you meet the contractor.

Company: _____

Representative Name: _____

Phone: _____

Email: _____

❏ How did you find out about this contractor?

❏ What services does this contractor offer?

❏ Is the contractor insured and bonded?

❏ Does the contractor have any specialties?

❏ What do the online reviews say about this contractor (see Google, Facebook, and the Better Business Bureau)?

Notes:

_____
_____
_____

Senior Planning Workbook

Contractor Questions (3.6)

(Before You Do the Work)

Directions: Fill this out before you meet the contractor.

Company: _____

Representative Name: _____

Phone: _____

Email: _____

❏ How did you find out about this contractor?

❏ What services does this contractor offer?

❏ Is the contractor insured and bonded?

❏ Does the contractor have any specialties?

❏ What do the online reviews say about this contractor (see Google, Facebook, and the Better Business Bureau)?

Notes:
_____
_____
_____

Home To Home

Contractor Questions (3.6)

(Before You Do the Work)

Directions: Fill this out before you meet the contractor.

Company: _____

Representative Name: _____

Phone: _____

Email: _____

❏ How did you find out about this contractor?

❏ What services does this contractor offer?

❏ Is the contractor insured and bonded?

❏ Does the contractor have any specialties?

❏ What do the online reviews say about this contractor (see Google, Facebook, and the Better Business Bureau)?

Notes:
_____
_____
_____

Contractor Questions (3.7)

(In Person)

Directions: Fill this out when you meet the contractor.

Company: _____

Representative Name: _____

Phone: _____

Email: _____

❑ What are the core values of your company?

❑ What kind of work do you specialize in?

❑ Do you perform background checks on your staff?

❑ How do you come up with your pricing?

❑ Do you have references I can call?

❑ When are you available to start work?

❑ What type of payment schedule do you follow?

Notes:
_____
_____
_____

Home To Home

Contractor Questions (3.7)

(In Person)

Directions: Fill this out when you meet the contractor.

Company: _____

Representative Name: _____

Phone: _____

Email: _____

❏ What are the core values of your company?

❏ What kind of work do you specialize in?

❏ Do you perform background checks on your staff?

❏ How do you come up with your pricing?

❏ Do you have references I can call?

❏ When are you available to start work?

❏ What type of payment schedule do you follow?

Notes:

_____
_____
_____

Senior Planning Workbook

Contractor Questions (3.7)

(In Person)

Directions: Fill this out when you meet the contractor.

Company: _____

Representative Name: _____

Phone: _____

Email: _____

❏ What are the core values of your company?

❏ What kind of work do you specialize in?

❏ Do you perform background checks on your staff?

❏ How do you come up with your pricing?

❏ Do you have references I can call?

❏ When are you available to start work?

❏ What type of payment schedule do you follow?

Notes:

_____

_____

_____

Home To Home

Contractor Questions (3.7)

(In Person)

Directions: Fill this out when you meet the contractor.

Company: _____

Representative Name: _____

Phone: _____

Email: _____

❏ What are the core values of your company?

❏ What kind of work do you specialize in?

❏ Do you perform background checks on your staff?

❏ How do you come up with your pricing?

❏ Do you have references I can call?

❏ When are you available to start work?

❏ What type of payment schedule do you follow?

Notes:

_____
_____
_____

Contractor Questions (3.7)

(In Person)

Directions: Fill this out when you meet the contractor.

Company: _____

Representative Name: _____

Phone: _____

Email: _____

❏ What are the core values of your company?

❏ What kind of work do you specialize in?

❏ Do you perform background checks on your staff?

❏ How do you come up with your pricing?

❏ Do you have references I can call?

❏ When are you available to start work?

❏ What type of payment schedule do you follow?

Notes:

_____
_____
_____

Investor Questions (3.8)

(Before You Do the Work)

Directions: Fill this out before you meet an investor-buyer.

☐ Are the mortgages, taxes, or any other liens late?

☐ Is there an impending foreclosure deadline?

☐ Is there a recent or impending bankruptcy?

☐ Is everyone on the title present and ready to sign the purchase agreement?

☐ Are there any family members or other advisors you want to include in this decision?

☐ What is the payoff amount for your mortgage?

☐ Come up with three prices for your home:

    ☐ Price you would really like   _____
    ☐ Price you would accept   _____
    ☐ Your absolute minimum price   _____

Senior Planning Workbook

Investor Questions (3.8)

(Before You Do the Work)

Directions: Fill this out before you meet an investor-buyer.

☐ Are the mortgages, taxes, or any other liens late?

☐ Is there an impending foreclosure deadline?

☐ Is there a recent or impending bankruptcy?

☐ Is everyone on the title present and ready to sign the purchase agreement?

☐ Are there any family members or other advisors you want to include in this decision?

☐ What is the payoff amount for your mortgage?

☐ Come up with three prices for your home:

    ☐ Price you would really like   _____
    ☐ Price you would accept   _____
    ☐ Your absolute minimum price   _____

Investor Questions (3.8)

(Before You Do the Work)

Directions: Fill this out before you meet an investor-buyer.

☐ Are the mortgages, taxes, or any other liens late?

☐ Is there an impending foreclosure deadline?

☐ Is there a recent or impending bankruptcy?

☐ Is everyone on the title present and ready to sign the purchase agreement?

☐ Are there any family members or other advisors you want to include in this decision?

☐ What is the payoff amount for your mortgage?

☐ Come up with three prices for your home:

    ☐ Price you would really like   _____
    ☐ Price you would accept   _____
    ☐ Your absolute minimum price   _____

Senior Planning Workbook

Investor Questions (3.8)

(Before You Do the Work)

Directions: Fill this out before you meet an investor-buyer.

☐ Are the mortgages, taxes, or any other liens late?

☐ Is there an impending foreclosure deadline?

☐ Is there a recent or impending bankruptcy?

☐ Is everyone on the title present and ready to sign the purchase agreement?

☐ Are there any family members or other advisors you want to include in this decision?

☐ What is the payoff amount for your mortgage?

☐ Come up with three prices for your home:

    ☐ Price you would really like   _____
    ☐ Price you would accept   _____
    ☐ Your absolute minimum price   _____

Investor Questions (3.8)

(Before You Do the Work)

Directions: Fill this out before you meet an investor-buyer.

☐ Are the mortgages, taxes, or any other liens late?

☐ Is there an impending foreclosure deadline?

☐ Is there a recent or impending bankruptcy?

☐ Is everyone on the title present and ready to sign the purchase agreement?

☐ Are there any family members or other advisors you want to include in this decision?

☐ What is the payoff amount for your mortgage?

☐ Come up with three prices for your home:

    ☐ Price you would really like   _____
    ☐ Price you would accept   _____
    ☐ Your absolute minimum price   _____

Senior Planning Workbook

Investor Questions (3.9)

(In Person)

Directions: Fill this out when you meet with the investor-buyer.

☐ How did you come up with a fair price for the home?

☐ How are you going to pay for the house? Do you have a proof-of-funds letter?

☐ If I perform repairs on the house, will that increase the value of the home?

☐ In what condition can we leave the house in if we sell it to you?

☐ When can we close?

☐ Do you have any references?

☐ Will you need access to the property?

☐ When will the utilities and insurance be cut off?

☐ What does the closing process look like?

☐ Who pays additional lawyer or closing costs?

Investor Questions (3.9)

(In Person)

Directions: Fill this out when you meet with the investor-buyer.

- ☐ How did you come up with a fair price for the home?

- ☐ How are you going to pay for the house? Do you have a proof-of-funds letter?

- ☐ If I perform repairs on the house, will that increase the value of the home?

- ☐ In what condition can we leave the house in if we sell it to you?

- ☐ When can we close?

- ☐ Do you have any references?

- ☐ Will you need access to the property?

- ☐ When will the utilities and insurance be cut off?

- ☐ What does the closing process look like?

- ☐ Who pays additional lawyer or closing costs?

Investor Questions (3.9)

(In Person)

Directions: Fill this out when you meet with the investor-buyer.

- ☐ How did you come up with a fair price for the home?

- ☐ How are you going to pay for the house? Do you have a proof-of-funds letter?

- ☐ If I perform repairs on the house, will that increase the value of the home?

- ☐ In what condition can we leave the house in if we sell it to you?

- ☐ When can we close?

- ☐ Do you have any references?

- ☐ Will you need access to the property?

- ☐ When will the utilities and insurance be cut off?

- ☐ What does the closing process look like?

- ☐ Who pays additional lawyer or closing costs?

Investor Questions (3.9)

(In Person)

Directions: Fill this out when you meet with the investor-buyer.

- ☐ How did you come up with a fair price for the home?

- ☐ How are you going to pay for the house? Do you have a proof-of-funds letter?

- ☐ If I perform repairs on the house, will that increase the value of the home?

- ☐ In what condition can we leave the house in if we sell it to you?

- ☐ When can we close?

- ☐ Do you have any references?

- ☐ Will you need access to the property?

- ☐ When will the utilities and insurance be cut off?

- ☐ What does the closing process look like?

- ☐ Who pays additional lawyer or closing costs?

Senior Planning Workbook

Investor Questions (3.9)

(In Person)

Directions: Fill this out when you meet with the investor-buyer.

- ☐ How did you come up with a fair price for the home?

- ☐ How are you going to pay for the house? Do you have a proof-of-funds letter?

- ☐ If I perform repairs on the house, will that increase the value of the home?

- ☐ In what condition can we leave the house in if we sell it to you?

- ☐ When can we close?

- ☐ Do you have any references?

- ☐ Will you need access to the property?

- ☐ When will the utilities and insurance be cut off?

- ☐ What does the closing process look like?

- ☐ Who pays additional lawyer or closing costs?

Home To Home

Keeping Your Home Questions (4.1)

(Before You Start Work)

☐ Have there been any recent event(s) that make keeping your home a concern or a challenge?

☐ If your health condition changes, how would you be able to stay in your home? What alterations would need to be made to your home?

☐ Do any family members want to buy your home? If so, who?

☐ If someone in the family wants to buy the home if it was to come up for sale, how will that person pay for the home?

☐ If the person plans on getting a mortgage to pay for your house, are they certain they will qualify for a loan?

☐ If your health changes and you lose mobility, who will maintain your home?

Monthly Home Budget (4.2)

Directions: Fill in the information to calculate your current home budget.

Address _____

Bedrooms _____   Bathrooms _____   Garage _____

Square Feet _____   Year Built _____

Yard Size (circle one) small   medium   large

Current Value of Home		Interest Rate
1st Mortgage Loan		
2nd Mortgage Loan		
Condition (circle one)	Good – Average – Poor	
Expenses – Monthly	Typical Monthly Cost	Actual Monthly Cost
1st Mortgage Payment	Based on loan amount	
2nd Mortgage Payment	Based on loan amount	
Homeowners Insurance	1% of the home value/12	
Property Taxes	1%–3% of home value/12	
Maintenance	1%–3% of home value/12	
HOA Fees	$0–$100+	
Utilities – Electric	$50–$250+	
Utilities – Gas	$25–$150+	
Utilities – Water	$25–$125+	
Utilities – Trash	$10–$40+	
Snow Removal	$0–$50+	
Lawn Care	$0–$150+	
	Total Monthly Budget	

Home To Home

Monthly Home Budget (4.2)

Directions: Fill in the information to calculate your current home budget.

Address _____

Bedrooms _____ Bathrooms _____ Garage _____

Square Feet _____ Year Built _____

Yard Size (circle one) small   medium   large

Current Value of Home		Interest Rate	
1st Mortgage Loan			
2nd Mortgage Loan			
Condition (circle one)	Good – Average – Poor		
Expenses - Monthly	Typical Monthly Cost	Actual Monthly Cost	
1st Mortgage Payment	Based on loan amount		
2nd Mortgage Payment	Based on loan amount		
Homeowners Insurance	1% of the home value/12		
Property Taxes	1%–3% of home value/12		
Maintenance	1%–3% of home value/12		
HOA Fees	$0–$100+		
Utilities – Electric	$50–$250+		
Utilities – Gas	$25–$150+		
Utilities – Water	$25–$125+		
Utilities – Trash	$10–$40+		
Snow Removal	$0–$50+		
Lawn Care	$0–$150+		
	Total Monthly Budget		

Senior Planning Workbook

Maintaining Major Home Systems (4.3)

Directions: Fill in the blanks below to calculate your projected costs.

Major Systems	Roof	Foundation Repair	Plumbing	Electrical	HVAC
Year Installed?					
How Old Is the Current System? (Current Year – Year installed)					
Estimated Lifespan	10–20 years	20–40 years	20–40 years	20–40 years	8–12 years
Years Left? (Life Span – Age of System)					
Estimated Cost	($6,000–$12,000)	($4,000–$10,000+)	($1,500–$10,000)	($2,000–$7,000)	($6,000–$10,000)
Items That May Need Replacement	Roof shingles	Foundation stabilization	Old water lines	Breaker box	Evaporator coil
Items That May Need Replacement	Decking	Outside brick	Sewer pipe	Aluminum wiring	Inside/Outside unit
Items That May Need Replacement	Water damage	Wall sheetrock	Hot water heater		Ductwork
Systems That Have Less Than Five Years Left (enter total)					
Projected Costs					

Maintaining Major Home Systems (4.3)

Directions: Fill in the blanks below to calculate your projected costs.

Major Systems	Roof	Foundation Repair	Plumbing	Electrical	HVAC
Year Installed?					
How Old Is the Current System? (Current Year – Year installed)					
Estimated Lifespan	10–20 years	20–40 years	20–40 years	20–40 years	8–12 years
Years Left? (Life Span – Age of System)					
Estimated Cost	($6,000–$12,000)	($4,000–$10,000+)	($1,500–$10,000)	($2,000–$7,000)	($6,000–$10,000)
Items That May Need Replacement	Roof shingles	Foundation stabilization	Old water lines	Breaker box	Evaporator coil
Items That May Need Replacement	Decking	Outside brick	Sewer pipe	Aluminum wiring	Inside/Outside unit
Items That May Need Replacement	Water damage	Wall sheetrock	Hot water heater		Ductwork
Systems That Have Less Than Five Years Left (enter total)					
Projected Costs					

153

Senior Planning Workbook

Contractor Referral Check Questions (4.4)

Name: _____

Phone: _____

Email: _____

☐ When did this contractor perform work at your home?

☐ What work did this contractor do for you?

☐ How did you like the completed job?

☐ Did the contractor get the work done on budget (time and money)?

☐ Would you recommend this contractor to someone else? Why or why not?

Notes:
_____
_____
_____

Home To Home

Contractor Referral Check Questions (4.4)

Name: _____

Phone: _____

Email: _____

☐ When did this contractor perform work at your home?

☐ What work did this contractor do for you?

☐ How did you like the completed job?

☐ Did the contractor get the work done on budget (time and money)?

☐ Would you recommend this contractor to someone else? Why or why not?

Notes:
_____
_____
_____

Senior Planning Workbook

Contractor Referral Check Questions (4.4)

Name: _____

Phone: _____

Email: _____

☐ When did this contractor perform work at your home?

☐ What work did this contractor do for you?

☐ How did you like the completed job?

☐ Did the contractor get the work done on budget (time and money)?

☐ Would you recommend this contractor to someone else? Why or why not?

Notes:
_____
_____
_____

Home To Home

Contractor Referral Check Questions (4.4)

Name: _____

Phone: _____

Email: _____

☐ When did this contractor perform work at your home?

☐ What work did this contractor do for you?

☐ How did you like the completed job?

☐ Did the contractor get the work done on budget (time and money)?

☐ Would you recommend this contractor to someone else? Why or why not?

Notes:

_____

_____

_____

Senior Planning Workbook

Contractor Referral Check Questions (4.4)

Name: _____

Phone: _____

Email: _____

☐ When did this contractor perform work at your home?

☐ What work did this contractor do for you?

☐ How did you like the completed job?

☐ Did the contractor get the work done on budget (time and money)?

☐ Would you recommend this contractor to someone else? Why or why not?

Notes:
_____
_____
_____

Home To Home

Contractor Tips (4.5)

☐ Was the job completed three weeks ago or three years ago? If it is a recent referral, even better.

☐ Make sure that the work you need done is something they have completed in the past. Contractors will sometimes say that they do certain work, but it is not really their specialty.

☐ If they would not recommend the contractor to somebody else, that contractor is probably not the right person for you.

☐ What happens if the work is not completed on time? You can request a penalty of $50 per day if work is not completed by a certain deadline; you can also provide an incentive for finishing early.

Notes:
_____
_____
_____

Contractor Tips (4.5)

☐ Was the job completed three weeks ago or three years ago? If it is a recent referral, even better.

☐ Make sure the work you need done is something they have completed in the past. Contractors will sometimes say that they do certain work, but it is not really their specialty.

☐ If they would not recommend the contractor to somebody else, that contractor is probably not the right person for you.

☐ What happens if the work is not completed on time? You can request a penalty of $50 per day if work is not completed by a certain deadline; you can also provide an incentive for finishing early.

Notes:
_____
_____
_____

Contractor Tips (4.5)

☐ Was the job completed three weeks ago or three years ago? If it is a recent referral, even better.

☐ Make sure the work you need done is something they have completed in the past. Contractors will sometimes say that they do certain work, but it is not really their specialty.

☐ If they would not recommend the contractor to somebody else, that contractor is probably not the right person for you.

☐ What happens if the work is not completed on time? You can request a penalty of $50 per day if work is not completed by a certain deadline; you can also provide an incentive for finishing early.

Notes:
_____
_____
_____

Contractor Tips (4.5)

☐ Was the job completed three weeks ago or three years ago? If it is a recent referral, even better.

☐ Make sure the work you need done is something they have completed in the past. Contractors will sometimes say that they do certain work, but it is not really their specialty.

☐ If they would not recommend the contractor to somebody else, that contractor is probably not the right person for you.

☐ What happens if the work is not completed on time? You can request a penalty of $50 per day if work is not completed by a certain deadline; you can also provide an incentive for finishing early.

Notes:
_____
_____
_____

Home To Home

Contractor Tips (4.5)

☐ Was the job completed three weeks ago or three years ago? If it is a recent referral, even better.

☐ Make sure the work you need done is something they have completed in the past. Contractors will sometimes say that they do certain work, but it is not really their specialty.

☐ If they would not recommend the contractor to somebody else, that contractor is probably not the right person for you.

☐ What happens if the work is not completed on time? You can request a penalty of $50 per day if work is not completed by a certain deadline; you can also provide an incentive for finishing early.

Notes:
_____
_____
_____

Senior Planning Workbook

Home Agency Phone Interview Questions (4.6)

Company: _____

Representative Name: _____

Phone: _____

Email: _____

☐ What services do you provide?

☐ How long have you been providing these services?

☐ Are you licensed by the state?

☐ Do you perform background checks on your staff?

☐ How will you communicate with my family members if needed?

☐ Are your caregivers available 24 hours a day?

☐ What type of fee structure do you have?

Notes:

_____

_____

_____

Home Agency Phone Interview Questions (4.6)

Company: _____

Representative Name: _____

Phone: _____

Email: _____

☐ What services do you provide?

☐ How long have you been providing these services?

☐ Are you licensed by the state?

☐ Do you perform background checks on your staff?

☐ How will you communicate with my family members if needed?

☐ Are your caregivers available 24 hours a day?

☐ What type of fee structure do you have?

Notes:
_____
_____
_____

Senior Planning Workbook

Home Agency Phone Interview Questions (4.6)

Company: _____

Representative Name: _____

Phone: _____

Email: _____

☐ What services do you provide?

☐ How long have you been providing these services?

☐ Are you licensed by the state?

☐ Do you perform background checks on your staff?

☐ How will you communicate with my family members if needed?

☐ Are your caregivers available 24 hours a day?

☐ What type of fee structure do you have?

Notes:

_____

_____

Home To Home

Home Agency Phone Interview Questions (4.6)

Company: _____

Representative Name: _____

Phone: _____

Email: _____

☐ What services do you provide?

☐ How long have you been providing these services?

☐ Are you licensed by the state?

☐ Do you perform background checks on your staff?

☐ How will you communicate with my family members if needed?

☐ Are your caregivers available 24 hours a day?

☐ What type of fee structure do you have?

Notes:
_____
_____
_____

Senior Planning Workbook

Home Agency Phone Interview Questions (4.6)

Company: _____

Representative Name: _____

Phone: _____

Email: _____

☐ What services do you provide?

☐ How long have you been providing these services?

☐ Are you licensed by the state?

☐ Do you perform background checks on your staff?

☐ How will you communicate with my family members if needed?

☐ Are your caregivers available 24 hours a day?

☐ What type of fee structure do you have?

Notes:
_____
_____
_____

Setting Up Your Plan (6.1)

Note: The following questions may be similar to the ones you answered in Chapter 2. Please answer them fully because your answers will reflect the knowledge you have gained in the chapters covered since then.

❏ Are there any current problems or challenges you are facing?

❏ What is the single biggest problem you are trying to solve?

❏ How soon do you expect to move into a senior housing facility?

❏ What geographical location do you want to live in?

❏ Do you have a specific housing need right now? If so, what is it (i.e., independent, assisted, nursing, or specialty)?

❏ What has prompted you to start this search?

❏ Where do you currently live?

❏ How long will it take to sell your home and/or move?

❏ Who are the members of your advisory team (e.g., spouse, children, family members, pastor, medical team, or professionals)?

❏ Is your advisory team part of your planning process?

Setting Up Your Plan Cont. (6.1)

❏ If price were no object, where would you want to live?

❏ What type of environment do you want to live in (e.g., private, community, social, private room, shared room, private house, or first floor)?

❏ What amenities would you like to have available (e.g., entertainment, recreation, food, pool, classes, and transportation)?

❏ What types of personal care services do you need now or want to be available (e.g., dressing, mobility help, laundry, bathing, and food)?

❏ What type of medical care services do you need now or want to be available (e.g., treatments, specialty care, medicine, or diabetes care)?

Notes:
_____
_____
_____

Your Team (6.2)

Directions: List Your Professional Team and Contact Info	
Professional	**Contact Info**
Attorney:	
Financial Advisor:	
CPA:	
Medical Team:	
Medical Team:	
Other Advisor:	
Other Advisor:	

❏ Let us review your advisory team list from Chapter 2. Have there been any changes? If so, what are they?

❏ Are there any other needs or wants you have not mentioned yet that are important to you?

❏ What is important to the members of your advisory team? Ask them if you have not already, e.g., "I am creating a Senior Housing Plan that I expect to begin following (fill in the date, for example, next month, next year, or ten years). What is important to you?

❏ Ask your advisory team, "Is there anything else you want me to consider as I am creating my plan?"

Notes:

_____

_____

_____

Closest Advisor Questions (6.3)

❏ Do you have any concerns regarding my health, safety, and overall happiness?

❏ What problems or challenges are you facing as my top advisor?

❏ Is moving in with you or anyone else in our family an option?

Notes:
_____
_____
_____

Your Budget (6.4)

(**Note:** Some of these are a recap of what you may have answered in preceding chapters).

❏ Do you use a monthly budget?

❏ What monthly amount can you afford for senior housing and care expenses?

❏ What financial sources are available to pay for senior housing?

❏ If you do not need senior housing right now, have you inquired about long-term care insurance?

❏ Do you expect family members to help pay for your housing? If so, how much do they plan to contribute?

❏ If you plan to sell your home, how much do you expect to receive?

Notes:
_____
_____
_____

Senior Planning Workbook

Other Planning Questions (6.5)

❏ Are you married?

❏ Do you currently live with anyone else?

❏ If you move, where is your current house partner (e.g., friend, family, or spouse) going to live?

❏ If your spouse were to die before you, would you want to stay in your current home?

❏ Would you prefer to move into a facility that has all the care options available, from independent to nursing, or would you be fine moving to a new facility if you needed more care?

❏ Do you want to be close to a church or place of worship? Which one?

❏ Is there a friend or family member you want to live close to?

❏ If you are thinking about moving across the city, state, or country, will you need to find a new doctor or other professionals?

❏ If you are moving into a furnished facility, what is the plan for your current furniture and personal belongings?

Other Planning Questions Cont. (6.5)

❏ If you plan to give items from your home away to family members, have you let your family members know?

❏ Will you get input from your family members before giving them any of your personal belongings?

❏ When you give a family member or friend your personal belongings, are the items theirs to keep or are you just letting them store them for you?

❏ Will you need to rent a storage facility? If so, where?

❏ How will you know when it is time to make a decision?

Notes:

_____
_____
_____

Senior Planning Workbook

Before You Call Questions (Identify) (6.6)

Directions: Circle housing type and fill out contact information.		
Independent	**Assisted**	**Nursing**
Age-Restricted Community	Assisted Living – Corp.	Nursing Home
Senior Apartments	Residential Assisted Living	CCRC
Senior Townhomes	Memory Care	Other
Senior Garden Homes	Other	
Live with Family		
Rent or Rent Out Room		
Other		
Facility Name:		
Phone Number:		
Address:		
Website:	Email:	

❏ How did I find out about this facility?

❏ How many of my needs does this facility meet?

❏ How many of my wants does this facility meet?

❏ Does this facility have the level of care I may need in the future?

❏ What do the online reviews say about this facility (see Google, Facebook, and the Better Business Bureau)?

Before You Call Questions (Identify) (6.6)

Directions: Circle housing type and fill out contact information		
Independent	**Assisted**	**Nursing**
Age-Restricted Community	Assisted Living – Corp.	Nursing Home
Senior Apartments	Residential Assisted Living	CCRC
Senior Townhomes	Memory Care	Other
Senior Garden Homes	Other	
Live with Family		
Rent or Rent Out Room		
Other		
Facility Name:		
Phone Number:		
Address:		
Website:	Email:	

❑ How did I find out about this facility?

❑ How many of my needs does this facility meet?

❑ How many of my wants does this facility meet?

❑ Does this facility have the level of care I may need in the future?

❑ What do the online reviews say about this facility (see Google, Facebook, and the Better Business Bureau)?

Senior Planning Workbook

Before You Call Questions (Identify) (6.6)

Directions: Circle housing type and fill out contact information		
Independent	Assisted	Nursing
Age-Restricted Community	Assisted Living – Corp.	Nursing Home
Senior Apartments	Residential Assisted Living	CCRC
Senior Townhomes	Memory Care	Other
Senior Garden Homes	Other	
Live with Family		
Rent or Rent Out Room		
Other		
Facility Name:		
Phone Number:		
Address:		
Website:	Email:	

❑ How did I find out about this facility?

❑ How many of my needs does this facility meet?

❑ How many of my wants does this facility meet?

❑ Does this facility have the level of care I may need in the future?

❑ What do the online reviews say about this facility (see Google, Facebook, and the Better Business Bureau)?

Home To Home

Before You Call Questions (Identify) (6.6)

Directions: Circle housing type and fill out contact information		
Independent	**Assisted**	**Nursing**
Age-Restricted Community	Assisted Living – Corp.	Nursing Home
Senior Apartments	Residential Assisted Living	CCRC
Senior Townhomes	Memory Care	Other
Senior Garden Homes	Other	
Live with Family		
Rent or Rent Out Room		
Other		
Facility Name:		
Phone Number:		
Address:		
Website:	Email:	

❏ How did I find out about this facility?

❏ How many of my needs does this facility meet?

❏ How many of my wants does this facility meet?

❏ Does this facility have the level of care I may need in the future?

❏ What do the online reviews say about this facility (see Google, Facebook, and the Better Business Bureau)?

Senior Planning Workbook

Before You Call Questions (Identify) (6.6)

Directions: Circle housing type and fill out contact information		
Independent	**Assisted**	**Nursing**
Age-Restricted Community	Assisted Living – Corp.	Nursing Home
Senior Apartments	Residential Assisted Living	CCRC
Senior Townhomes	Memory Care	Other
Senior Garden Homes	Other	
Live with Family		
Rent or Rent Out Room		
Other		
Facility Name:		
Phone Number:		
Address:		
Website:	Email:	

❏ How did I find out about this facility?

❏ How many of my needs does this facility meet?

❏ How many of my wants does this facility meet?

❏ Does this facility have the level of care I may need in the future?

❏ What do the online reviews say about this facility (see Google, Facebook, and the Better Business Bureau)?

Call the Facility (Phone Interview) (6.7)

Directions: Fill out contact information and answers to all questions.	
Facility:	Phone #:
Talked to:	Date/Time:

❏ Do you have any openings at your facility?

❏ What services do you provide?

❏ Do you perform background checks on your staff? What about the residents?

❏ Is your facility accredited? If so, with whom?

❏ How much should I budget for if I move into your facility (not an exact number, just a range)?

❏ If I become a resident, how often do rates change?

❏ What is the best way that I can get more information about your facility?

❏ When can I take a tour of the facility and learn more?

Call the Facility (Phone Interview) (6.7)

Directions: Fill out contact information and answers to all questions.	
Facility:	Phone #:
Talked to:	Date/Time:

❏ Do you have any openings at your facility?

❏ What services do you provide?

❏ Do you perform background checks on your staff? What about the residents?

❏ Is your facility accredited? If so, with whom?

❏ How much should I budget for if I move into your facility (not an exact number, just a range)?

❏ If I become a resident, how often do rates change?

❏ What is the best way that I can get more information about your facility?

❏ When can I take a tour of the facility and learn more?

Home To Home

Call the Facility (Phone Interview) (6.7)

Directions: Fill out contact information and answers to all questions.	
Facility:	Phone #:
Talked to:	Date/Time:

❏ Do you have any openings at your facility?

❏ What services do you provide?

❏ Do you perform background checks on your staff? What about the residents?

❏ Is your facility accredited? If so, with whom?

❏ How much should I budget for if I move into your facility (not an exact number, just a range)?

❏ If I become a resident, how often do rates change?

❏ What is the best way that I can get more information about your facility?

❏ When can I take a tour of the facility and learn more?

Senior Planning Workbook

Call the Facility (Phone Interview) (6.7)

Directions: Fill out contact information and answers to all questions.	
Facility:	Phone #:
Talked to:	Date/Time:

❏ Do you have any openings at your facility?

❏ What services do you provide?

❏ Do you perform background checks on your staff? What about the residents?

❏ Is your facility accredited? If so, with whom?

❏ How much should I budget for if I move into your facility (not an exact number, just a range)?

❏ If I become a resident, how often do rates change?

❏ What is the best way that I can get more information about your facility?

❏ When can I take a tour of the facility and learn more?

Call the Facility (Phone Interview) (6.7)

Directions: Fill out contact information and answers to all questions.	
Facility:	Phone #:
Talked to:	Date/Time:

❑ Do you have any openings at your facility?

❑ What services do you provide?

❑ Do you perform background checks on your staff? What about the residents?

❑ Is your facility accredited? If so, with whom?

❑ How much should I budget for if I move into your facility (not an exact number, just a range)?

❑ If I become a resident, how often do rates change?

❑ What is the best way that I can get more information about your facility?

❑ When can I take a tour of the facility and learn more?

Senior Planning Workbook

Tour Questions (In Person Interview) (6.8)

Directions: Fill out contact information and answers to all questions.	
Facility:	Phone #:
Address:	
Talked to:	Date and Time:

❏ Ask your tour person how long they have worked there and what their main focus is.

❏ Who is the current manager or director? How long have they been there?

❏ What services are not offered here?

❏ What do you like about working here?

❏ What would you change about the facility if you could?

❏ Ask if you can speak to any other employees and residents about their experience at the facility.

❏ How do you communicate with family members?

❏ What are their visiting hours?

Home To Home

Tour Questions (In Person Interview) Cont. (6.8)

❑ Do they have any referrals of current residents or past residents/family members you can contact?

❑ Is this a for profit or non-profit facility? If you have experience with each one, what differences do you see in this one?

❑ If I were to move in today and order certain services, what would my price be?

❑ How often do rates change?

❑ How many openings do you have right now?

❑ Is the rate open to negotiation? If so, under what circumstances?

❑ What is the application process? How long does it take?

❑ Are there any questions I should have asked that I did not?

❑ How long can we take to make a decision?

Senior Planning Workbook

Tour Questions (In Person Interview) (6.8)

Directions: Fill out contact information and answers to all questions.	
Facility:	Phone #:
Address:	
Talked to:	Date and Time:

❏ Ask your tour person how long they have worked there and what their main focus is.

❏ Who is the current manager or director? How long have they been there?

❏ What services are not offered here?

❏ What do you like about working here?

❏ What would you change about the facility if you could?

❏ Ask if you can speak to any other employees and residents about their experience at the facility.

❏ How do you communicate with family members?

❏ What are their visiting hours?

Home To Home

Tour Questions (In Person Interview) Cont. (6.8)

❏ Do they have any referrals of current residents or past residents/family members you can contact?

❏ Is this a for profit or non-profit facility? If you have experience with each one, what differences do you see in this one?

❏ If I were to move in today and order certain services, what would my price be?

❏ How often do rates change?

❏ How many openings do you have right now?

❏ Is the rate open to negotiation? If so, under what circumstances?

❏ What is the application process? How long does it take?

❏ Are there any questions I should have asked that I did not?

❏ How long can we take to make a decision?

Senior Planning Workbook

Tour Questions (In Person Interview) (6.8)

Directions: Fill out contact information and answers to all questions.	
Facility:	Phone #:
Address:	
Talked to:	Date and Time:

❏ Ask your tour person how long they have worked there and what their main focus is.

❏ Who is the current manager or director? How long have they been there?

❏ What services are not offered here?

❏ What do you like about working here?

❏ What would you change about the facility if you could?

❏ Ask if you can speak to any other employees and residents about their experience at the facility.

❏ How do you communicate with family members?

❏ What are their visiting hours?

Tour Questions (In Person Interview) Cont. (6.8)

❏ Do they have any referrals of current residents or past residents/family members you can contact?

❏ Is this a for profit or non-profit facility? If you have experience with each one, what differences do you see in this one?

❏ If I were to move in today and order certain services, what would my price be?

❏ How often do rates change?

❏ How many openings do you have right now?

❏ Is the rate open to negotiation? If so, under what circumstances?

❏ What is the application process? How long does it take?

❏ Are there any questions I should have asked that I did not?

❏ How long can we take to make a decision?

Senior Planning Workbook

Tour Questions (In Person Interview) (6.8)

Directions: Fill out contact information and answers to all questions.	
Facility:	Phone #:
Address:	
Talked to:	Date and Time:

❏ Ask your tour person how long they have worked there and what their main focus is.

❏ Who is the current manager or director? How long have they been there?

❏ What services are not offered here?

❏ What do you like about working here?

❏ What would you change about the facility if you could?

❏ Ask if you can speak to any other employees and residents about their experience at the facility.

❏ How do you communicate with family members?

❏ What are their visiting hours?

Tour Questions (In Person Interview) Cont. (6.8)

❏ Do they have any referrals of current residents or past residents/family members you can contact?

❏ Is this a for profit or non-profit facility? If you have experience with each one, what differences do you see in this one?

❏ If I were to move in today and order certain services, what would my price be?

❏ How often do rates change?

❏ How many openings do you have right now?

❏ Is the rate open to negotiation? If so, under what circumstances?

❏ What is the application process? How long does it take?

❏ Are there any questions I should have asked that I did not?

❏ How long can we take to make a decision?

Senior Planning Workbook

Tour Questions (In Person Interview) (6.8)

Directions: Fill out contact information and answers to all questions.	
Facility:	Phone #:
Address:	
Talked to:	Date and Time:

❑ Ask your tour person how long they have worked there and what their main focus is.

❑ Who is the current manager or director? How long have they been there?

❑ What services are not offered here?

❑ What do you like about working here?

❑ What would you change about the facility if you could?

❑ Ask if you can speak to any other employees and residents about their experience at the facility.

❑ How do you communicate with family members?

❑ What are their visiting hours?

Tour Questions (In Person Interview) Cont. (6.8)

❏ Do they have any referrals of current residents or past residents/family members you can contact?

❏ Is this a for profit or non-profit facility? If you have experience with each one, what differences do you see in this one?

❏ If I were to move in today and order certain services, what would my price be?

❏ How often do rates change?

❏ How many openings do you have right now?

❏ Is the rate open to negotiation? If so, under what circumstances?

❏ What is the application process? How long does it take?

❏ Are there any questions I should have asked that I did not?

❏ How long can we take to make a decision?

Senior Planning Workbook

Facility Comparison Part 1 (6.9)

Directions: You invested time in researching, calling, and visiting different facilities — now it is time to rank your top two choices. Since different things are important to different people, you are going to customize your comparison checklist to what is most important to you.

Tip: Try to focus on the questions and not the answers received in Part 1 of this exercise.

Step 1: Review all the questions in the *Before You Call Checklist*.

What is the number one most important question to YOU on that checklist? Circle it.

Step 2: Review the questions on the *Call The Facility Checklist*.

What are the top two most important questions to YOU on that checklist? Circle them.

Step 3: Review the questions on the *Tour Questions Checklist*.

What are the top three most important questions to YOU on that checklist? Circle them.

Notes:
_____
_____
_____

Facility Comparison Part 1 (6.9)

Directions: You invested time in researching, calling, and visiting different facilities — now it is time to rank your top two choices. Since different things are important to different people, you are going to customize your comparison checklist to what is most important to you.

Tip: Try to focus on the questions and not the answers received in Part 1 of this exercise.

Step 1: Review all the questions in the *Before You Call Checklist*.

What is the number one most important question to YOU on that checklist? Circle it.

Step 2: Review the questions on the *Call The Facility Checklist*.

What are the top two most important questions to YOU on that checklist? Circle them.

Step 3: Review the questions on the *Tour Questions Checklist*.

What are the top three most important questions to YOU on that checklist? Circle them.

Notes:
_____
_____
_____

Senior Planning Workbook

Facility Comparison Part 1 (6.9)

Directions: You invested time in researching, calling, and visiting different facilities — now it is time to rank your top two choices. Since different things are important to different people, you are going to customize your comparison checklist to what is most important to you.

Tip: Try to focus on the questions and not the answers received in Part 1 of this exercise.

Step 1: Review all the questions in the *Before You Call Checklist*.

What is the number one most important question to YOU on that checklist? Circle it.

Step 2: Review the questions on the *Call The Facility Checklist*.

What are the top two most important questions to YOU on that checklist? Circle them.

Step 3: Review the questions on the *Tour Questions Checklist*.

What are the top three most important questions to YOU on that checklist? Circle them.

Notes:
_____
_____
_____

Home To Home

Facility Comparison Part 1 (6.9)

Directions: You invested time in researching, calling, and visiting different facilities — now it is time to rank your top two choices. Since different things are important to different people, you are going to customize your comparison checklist to what is most important to you.

Tip: Try to focus on the questions and not the answers received in Part 1 of this exercise.

Step 1: Review all the questions in the *Before You Call Checklist*.

What is the number one most important question to YOU on that checklist? Circle it.

Step 2: Review the questions on the *Call The Facility Checklist.*

What are the top two most important questions to YOU on that checklist? Circle them.

Step 3: Review the questions on the *Tour Questions Checklist.*

What are the top three most important questions to YOU on that checklist? Circle them.

Notes:
_____
_____
_____

Senior Planning Workbook

Facility Comparison Part 1 (6.9)

Directions: You invested time in researching, calling, and visiting different facilities — now it is time to rank your top two choices. Since different things are important to different people, you are going to customize your comparison checklist to what is most important to you.

Tip: Try to focus on the questions and not the answers received in Part 1 of this exercise.

Step 1: Review all the questions in the *Before You Call Checklist*.

What is the number one most important question to YOU on that checklist? Circle it.

Step 2: Review the questions on the *Call The Facility Checklist.*

What are the top two most important questions to YOU on that checklist? Circle them.

Step 3: Review the questions on the *Tour Questions Checklist.*

What are the top three most important questions to YOU on that checklist? Circle them.

Notes:
_____
_____
_____

Facility Comparison Part 2 (6.10)

Directions: Write the names of your top two facilities. Write your top question(s) for each checklist on the left side of the table. Give each answer a score and total up each facility. Use the scoring guide at the bottom.

Facility Name (Top Two)		
Score	1–10	1–10
Before You Call Questions:		
Call the Facility Questions:		
Call the Facility Questions:		
Tour Questions:		
Tour Questions:		
Tour Questions:		
Total (total your six scores)		
Score: 60–48 = Great 47–42 = Average 41 and Below = No	Great Average No	Great Average No

Senior Planning Workbook

Facility Comparison Part 2 (6.10)

Directions: Write the names of your top two facilities. Write your top question(s) for each checklist on the left side of the table. Give each answer a score and total up each facility. Use the scoring guide at the bottom.

Facility Name (Top Two)		
Score	1–10	1–10
Before You Call Questions:		
Call the Facility Questions:		
Call the Facility Questions:		
Tour Questions:		
Tour Questions:		
Tour Questions:		
Total (total your six scores)		
Score: 60–48 = Great 47–42 = Average 41 and Below = No	Great Average No	Great Average No

202

Facility Comparison Part 2 (6.10)

Directions: Write the names of your top two facilities. Write your top question(s) for each checklist on the left side of the table. Give each answer a score and total up each facility. Use the scoring guide at the bottom.

Facility Name (Top Two)			
Score	1–10	1–10
Before You Call Questions:		
Call the Facility Questions:		
Call the Facility Questions:		
Tour Questions:		
Tour Questions:		
Tour Questions:		
Total (total your six scores)		
Score: 60–48 = Great 47–42 = Average 41 and Below = No	Great Average No	Great Average No

About Us
Brad and Christy Brewer

Brad and Christy have been married for 23 years but have 24 years of experience in the real estate industry. They left the corporate world behind them seven years ago to start their family-owned real estate company.

They pride themselves on their core values of honesty, dependability, and compassion, and are driven by a desire to help seniors in the community live the very best life they can. Taking inspiration from their faith, Brad and Christy aspire to follow Jesus' example, his ability to influence others through his words and actions and his unconditional love for all. They have made it their mission to be approachable and caring to others, their only desire being to impact on the lives of others positively. Both Brad and Christy are passionate about learning from their experiences and honing their ability to help others, implementing what they learn to better themselves and the services they provide.

In addition to their core values, Brad and Christy believe in making sure that they can lay their heads down at night in the knowledge they have done right by others during the day and sleep peacefully without any regrets. At the forefront of this are the qualities they believe are the building blocks for a happy and productive life: Honesty, strength of character, and hard work.

Both Brad and Christy demonstrate honesty in their approach to buying and selling properties, as they endeavor to provide clients with an unbiased opinion of what is in their best interests, regardless of whether it directly benefits Brad and Christy or not. In these interactions and their professional conduct, they like to ensure that their strong moral values shine through their personable and approachable demeanors. Brad and Christy like to end each day knowing they have done their very best for each of their clients.

Max Keller

Max knows how to teach and create success. Max went from being a full-time high school Math Teacher to creating multiple successful real estate and marketing businesses. He has published multiple books and currently licenses his lead generation systems to real estate professionals all over the country.

Although business is Max's new full-time obsession, one thing has never left... this heart of a teacher. Max loves the opportunity to teach, inspire, and share real-world applications that can transform the lives of business owners.

A few of his current roles are consultant, teacher, author, speaker, and expert panelist. He has flipped over 100 houses and is on a mission to help real estate professionals have customers chasing them.

Book Max to speak at your event at www.maxnkeller.com

Friend Max on Facebook: www.facebook.com/Max.N.Keller

Made in the USA
Middletown, DE
22 June 2020